AF571805

WATERCOLOR PORTRAITURE

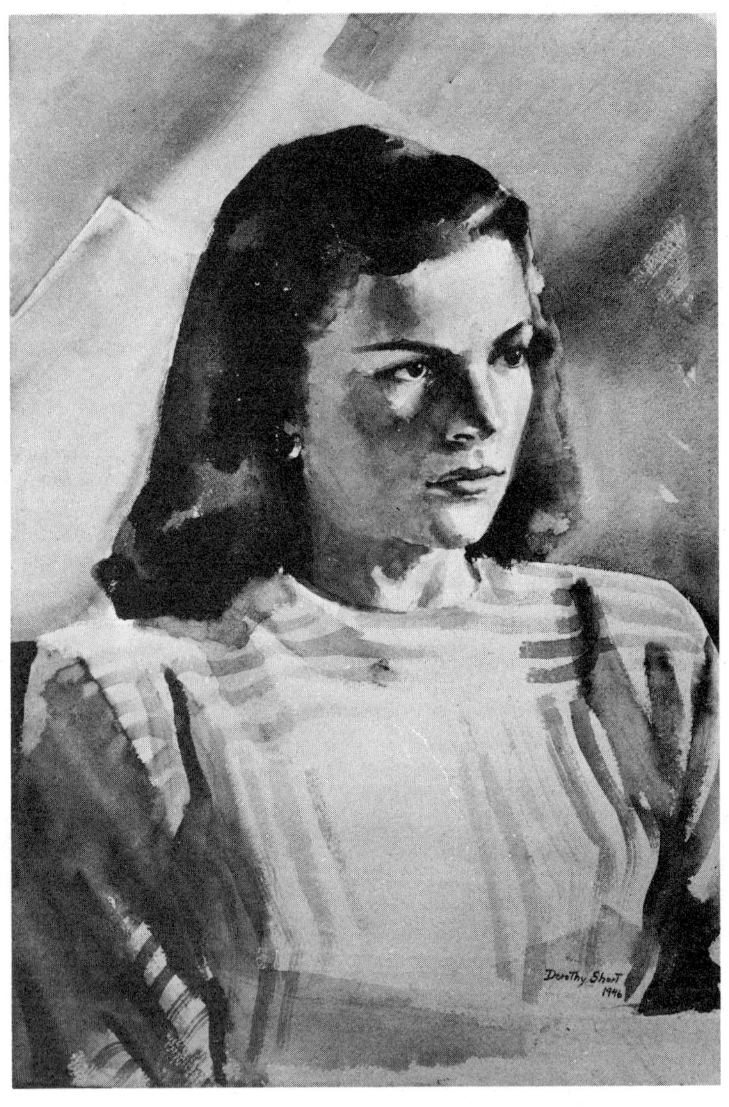

Dorothy Short: "Toni in Yellow" (Reproduced in color on the back cover.)

WATERCOLOR PORTRAITURE

A PRACTICAL GUIDE

BY

PHOEBE FLORY

with

DOROTHY SHORT PAUL

and ELIOT O'HARA

DOVER PUBLICATIONS, INC., NEW YORK

Copyright © 1949 by G. P. Putnam's Sons.
Copyright renewed © 1977 by Phoebe Flory, Dorothy Short Paul and Desmond O'Hara.
Copyright © 1985 by Phoebe Flory and Dorothy Short Paul.
All rights reserved under Pan American and International Copyright Conventions.

Published in Canada by General Publishing Company, Ltd., 30 Lesmill Road, Don Mills, Toronto, Ontario.
Published in the United Kingdom by Constable and Company, Ltd., 10 Orange Street, London WC2H 7EG.

This Dover edition, first published in 1985, is a revised republication of the work originally published by G. P. Putnam's Sons, New York, in 1949, as *Watercolor Portraiture*, by Phoebe Flory Walker, with Dorothy Short and Eliot O'Hara. The original section "A Suggested Reference List of Books for the Painter of Watercolor Portraits" is omitted from the present edition, and the frontispiece and Plates 3, 20 and 34, originally reproduced in color, are here reproduced in black and white in the text; the frontispiece and Plates 20 and 34 are reproduced in color on the covers.

Manufactured in the United States of America
Dover Publications, Inc., 31 East 2nd Street, Mineola, N.Y. 11501

Library of Congress Cataloging in Publication Data

Flory, Phoebe.
Watercolor portraiture.

Bibliography: p.
1. Portrait painting—Technique. 2. Watercolor painting—Technique. I. Paul, Dorothy Short. II. O'Hara, Eliot, 1890–1969. III. Title. IV. Title: Watercolor portraiture.
ND2200.F56 1985 751.42′242 85-12889
ISBN 0-486-24972-7

PREFACE TO THE DOVER EDITION

SINCE this book's publication in 1949 there have been several marked changes in the general art scene: the revived interest in recognizable subject matter, the increase in the use of and respect for watercolor, the return to people as primary subject matter, and the widespread popularity of painting as a leisure activity. It is too bad that Eliot O'Hara, who pioneered in teaching and writing about transparent watercolor, did not live to see some of the magnificent applications of his chosen medium being produced today. He would have applauded the variety of experiments in watercolor that have emerged since his death in 1969 and rejoiced in the boldness of their applications.

Aware of these changes, we, the two surviving authors, approached with uneasiness the critical rereading of our book in preparation for this republication. We are surprised, however, and rather pleased to find that the bulk of our teaching contained in this volume is still applicable. We, along with the publishers, believe that the material warrants being made available to contemporary painters.

Three chapters were contributed by guest artists. Carl N. Schmalz has made a few revisions in his. The writers of the other two guest chapters are no longer living.

There are many topics we touched upon in 1949 that we would now like to expand, and whole new topics—such as working from photographs and a new reading list—that we wish we could include, but which must await another publication. Aside from the few changes we have made, the bulk of the volume is substantially as it appeared originally. May it contribute to your joy in painting!

P.F. and D.S.P.

CONTENTS

ILLUSTRATIONS

WATERCOLOR PORTRAITURE

CHAPTER I

STILL TIME TO PIONEER

EVEN AFTER being freed from the traditional nineteenth-century tightness and monotony of style, transparent watercolor remained for years "the medium of the amateur or the master." Schools avoided teaching it and exhibition galleries kept it relegated either to the print room or to the smallest and most poorly lighted space in the building.

"Happy accidents" were courted by some of the watercolorists, in the hope that a lucky break might supplement invention. A few, however, possessed enough boldness, skill, and imagination to carry out an intention without recourse to superimposed washes, scrubbing, or opaque overpainting. Among these were Winslow Homer and John Singer Sargent, and a small group of fellow enthusiasts in the medium.

By the twenties, greater numbers were exploring the field of direct painting in watercolor, and were bringing fluid washes and rough brushing under control. In the United States there was a growing vanguard of artists sure enough of their watercolor technique to risk making the medium their lifework. Demuth, Keller, Marin, Burchfield, Sheets, and Whorf were among the pioneers who were willing and eager to discard other mediums of expression in favor of watercolor, and who, whatever they may have turned to since, will go down in history primarily as watercolorists.

Their success gave the impetus that helped to turn more and more interest into a field that offered exciting new vistas. When, in the early thirties, more specific teaching became available for control of this versatile but elusive medium, students could study watercolor as seriously as they had oil. (Even today a watercolor is often not classified as a "painting." Yet a watercolor exhibit on Fifty-seventh Street has become a commonplace rather than a rarity.)

Any skill or art that requires at the same time manual dexterity and "know how" takes for granted a good grounding in fundamentals.

One of the great marvels of our time is the way in which training and properly disciplined co-ordination permit the breaking of athletic records year after year by persons of no greater strength or physical prowess than that possessed by last year's champions. If pole-vaulters can continually climb to greater heights, I am sure that there is no end to where the watercolorist may go, providing he gets even a little help from the trainer in techniques and in modes of interpretation. Mere discipline, however, will not carry him beyond the mediocre, unless he commands inner resources of courage and vision and uses these with integrity. He must know what he wishes to say, and care how it is said.

This schooling procedure has brought us to a point where almost anyone who is willing to study can learn to perform the various feats involved in the technical part of watercolor painting. He may exploit his knowledge of color mixtures, surface textures, and special effects in accordance with his capacities. Thoughts in him that want expression, whatever their level, can flow freely with little hindrance from mechanical obstructions or frantic use of synonyms when the right word eludes him.

We have long been familiar with the subtle and suggestive qualities of transparent watercolor. We are now learning what heights of clarity, boldness, and conviction it can reach, and in one lifetime have seen the medium take strong root and branch out in ever new directions. Many pictures that took prizes and brought high prices only ten years ago would not be hung in most of our major watercolor exhibitions today. This is usually due not, as one might expect, to failure in meeting the changes from realistic to more subjective approaches. The rejection is more often on the grounds of inability to meet a higher painting standard.

Although watercolor landscape, still life, and abstraction are in great supply, there is one field into which the medium has not ventured far. That is portraiture.

While there have been a few examples of watercolor figure pieces and portraits, they are seldom done—as was true twenty years ago with landscape—in single transparent washes. One reason for this is because few watercolorists have learned to achieve a likeness. Most of the oil or pastel portraitists converting to watercolor, moreover, bring with them habits of scumbling, of overlaying mistakes with thick body color, or of building up values by a series of washes. Other artists produce pencil or charcoal drawings filled in with light watercolor washes, such as Holbein's portrait of Sir John Godsalve, Plate 1.

Like the pole-vaulters, who have been able to make new records by dint of practice, we can attempt to train ourselves to meet this latest challenge open to direct water color painting.

The author of this book and the two collaborators had for some time tried occasional watercolor portraits, with the usual uneven results. Four years ago they decided to experiment with specific procedures, directed toward producing more consistently fresh and vital portraits. The problem was to reduce the accidental, so far as possible, and to obviate inept repair measures; then to devise ways of teaching this approach. Two chapters have been contributed by guest writers: Carl N. Schmalz Jr. offers a comprehensive essay on the staining and transparent paints; Mitchell Jamieson, expert in several mediums, discusses the use of colored inks. Biographies of each of them will be found at the back of the book.

This volume has grown out of the joint and separate experience of the three principal authors in painting and teaching watercolor, just as their preceding book, *Portraits in the Making,* developed through their efforts to evolve a systematic method for learning general portraiture. There, six guest authors also treated of the subject in different mediums: oil, pastel, watercolor, egg tempera, mixed egg tempera and oil technique, and encaustic. In this book, the painter's training is built up, step by step, from the elementals of watercolor technique to its more elaborate application in various styles of portraiture.

All the materials for a watercolor portrait can be carried in a knapsack; and since there is no mess or odor about the job, the sittings can take place wherever the client feels most at home. Although it is a fact not generally recognized, good watercolor paint on the best rag paper provides one of the most permanent mediums.

The short time required for a watercolor portrait (rarely more than an hour and a half) means that both your sitter and you will easily sustain your initial interest.

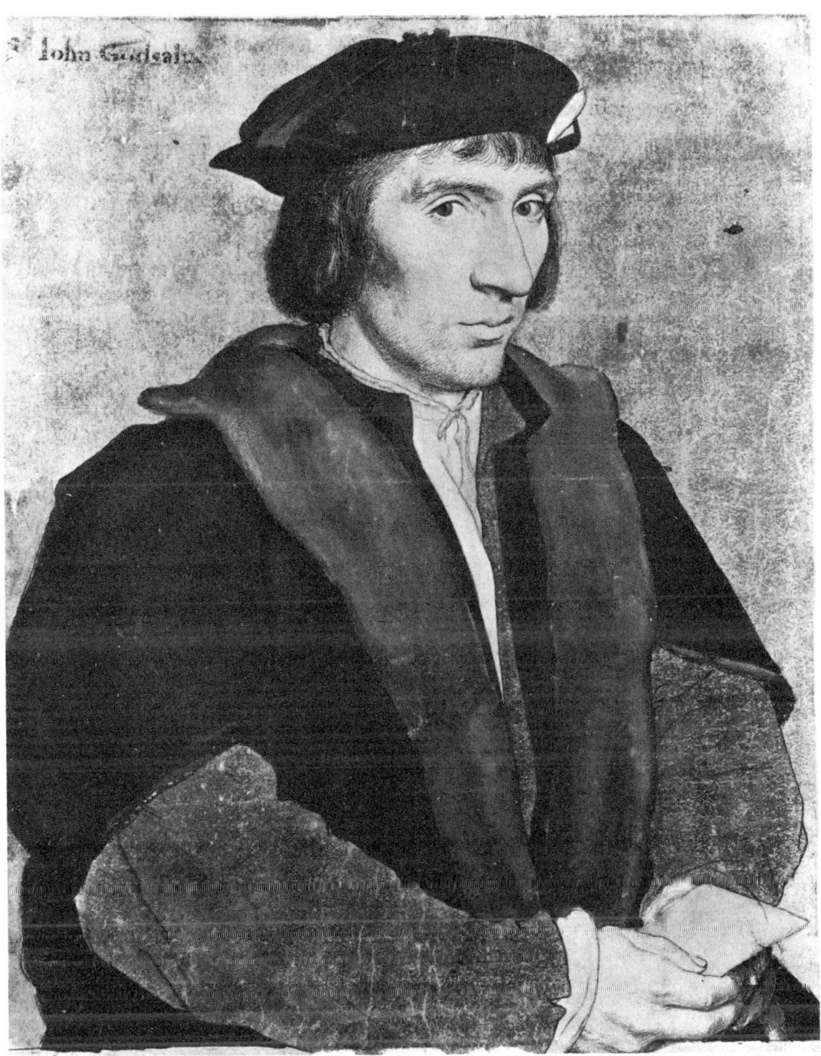

PLATE 1. Hans Holbein the Younger: "Sir John Godsalve" (India ink with watercolor and body-color). A watercolor study was sometimes made by Holbein for a subsequent oil portrait. *In the Royal Collection, Windsor Castle, reproduced by gracious permission of H.M. The King.*

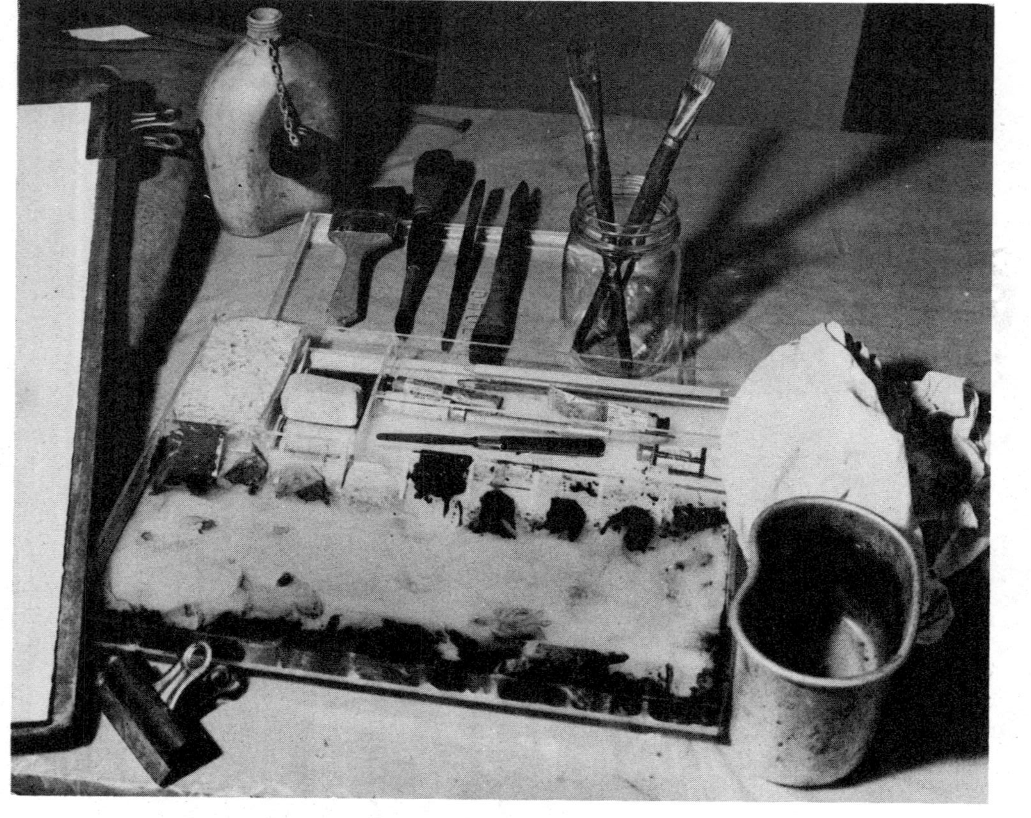

PLATE 2. Tools of the Trade. Metal, porcelain, or plastic palette, round or flat brushes, and other equipment, conveniently arranged.

Even if you have to try three or four times, you are still well within the period consumed by the painter in a more tedious medium. It is also true that, by working rapidly one retains the elusive resemblance often acquired early but sometimes painted out when more sittings are required.

When you are able to produce a watercolor portrait with confidence, not only will you have the satisfaction of helping to pioneer this profession, but you will become convinced that the versatility, speed, and incisiveness of watercolor makes it a medium singularly appropriate to portraiture.

E.O'H.

CHAPTER II

EQUIPMENT AND ITS CARE AND STORAGE

AS THE artist develops his technique he will constantly be discovering new tools and discarding others, taking care never to accumulate so much that it confuses rather than simplifies his work. The items listed below as a starter are merely suggestions. You may be accustomed to different materials that will do just as well.

Pencil. Soft (4B or 6B).

Eraser. Art gum, kneaded, soft plastic, or whatever cleans without damaging the paper.

Paper. A paper made with 100-per-cent rag content is the most permanent. Cheaper papers that contain wood pulp turn yellow with age. The 140-pound weight can be used without stretching, by clipping to a board. A lighter-weight paper will not buckle if used with a very dry technique, such as rough brushing. Blocked paper will not remain flat enough when wet. While it is possible to stretch the paper on a board or on oil canvas stretchers, this reduces the roughness required in some techniques.

Four bulldog clips. Better than thumbtacks, since they can be adjusted as the paper expands when it is moistened.

Board. Prestwood, ⅛-inch thick, is light in weight and thin enough to permit clips, about one inch wider and longer than paper to be used.

Several clean rags.

Water. For studio work: a jar or bowl. Some painters

set a jar (for fresh painting water) within a larger bowl (for rinsing brushes). Portable, for work away from the artist's studio: a screw-top jar, or nonbreakables such as an army canteen with cup, hot-water bottle, or ice pack.

Brushes. 1-inch flat-stroke brush, sable, ox hair, sablene, or nylon (camel hair is too limp), with hairs about ¾-inch from ferrule to tip. Some come with a plastic handle shaped into a scraping tool. The illustration, Plate 2, shows, standing in the jar, a short-haired and a long-haired brush, both 1 inch wide. (Their widths are foreshortened in the photograph.)

½-inch flat brush.

Rigger or liner, a long-haired, pointed brush good for drawing.

Round pointed brush, size number 8 or 9.

Optional:

2-inch flat brush, camel hair or nylon.

Round pointed brush, size 8 or 9, with a blunt tip, or an old worn-down pointed brush is good.

1¼-inch flat-stroke brush. In the illustration, this brush is shown (next to the 2-inch camel hair) combined with a large pointed brush. Next to it is the ½-inch sable combined with a number 8 pointed one.

Paint box. For tube colors, with a palette and place for brushes, pencil, eraser, knife, etc. The box shown in the illustration is made of ⅛-inch plastic, about 11½ by 14½ inches and 1 inch deep. The bottom, of "milk white" or translucent plastic, forms a palette which (unlike an enameled or painted metal box) cannot be stained by the dye paints. We also recommend an aluminum box, about 12 by 6 inches and 1 inch deep, with a removable paint tray. If you lack a box, substitute with:

Palette. Preferably white, on which the colors will approximate the effect of the paint mixtures on white paper.

Brush holder. Sign painter's metal brush holder or one made of rolled up cardboard (or paper-towel roll, or mailing tube) sealed at one end with sticky tape.

Small box for tube colors and eraser.

Instrument for knifing. The illustration shows two types: a blunt paring knife is strapped to the handle of one of the flat-stroke brushes (to the left of the jar); in the box (next to the palette knife) is an orangewood sculptor's tool, carved to the proper shape and affixed into a metal "pencil extender."

Tubes of paint. See the next two chapters entitled "A Watercolor Palette" and "A Staining and Transparent Palette." The entire palette pictured here was mixed from the four colors mentioned in Chapter IV, in quantities sufficient to last several months. They are kept moist by the dampened sponge shown in the far left compartment. It should be warned, however, that if the wet sponge is used the eraser should be kept wrapped to remain dry; and unless the box is in constant use, there is the chance of mildew. Dye colors retain their moisture longer and can be redampened more successfully than pigments.

Palette knife. For mixing the staining and transparent colors.

Mirror. Useful for checking mistakes in the portrait, by reversing the image and reducing its size. (Shown in the illustration under the eraser.)

Sheet of plastic, newspapers, oilcloth, or canvas, to protect a table or rug from stray drops of paint in the sitter's home. Can be folded into:

Bag or knapsack. Large enough to carry everything in storage or in transit. During the drawing, and sometimes during the painting, it can be used, as in the illustration, to prop up the board, so that the artist will not get a foreshortened view of his portrait.

Folding stool. Optional. (At the time of the photograph, since the artist was working standing at a table, the stool was left in the knapsack to raise the board higher.) The painter who wishes to be lower than his model may sit on the stool with his paints on the floor or low table.

Watercolor easel. Optional. The best, but one hard to obtain, is the type in which the rack holding the board moves on a universal joint. The board can thus be tipped in any direction with but slight pressure. Next best is the kind with the rack controlled by a wing bolt. It tips from vertical to flat, and therefore can be used equally well for oil, pastel, or watercolor painting. Both types should have extension legs which enable the artist to paint sitting or standing. Since a table is necessary anyhow (for the water and paints) it is usually easier to dispense with the easel. A lightweight adjustable ironing board makes a good studio painting table.

Keep your equipment down to the minimum. Do not arrive at your sitter's home with a vanload of gear.

CARE AND STORAGE

Paper. Store paper flat, covered to keep it clean, and in a dry atmosphere. If exposed to a moist atmosphere for considerable time it is apt to mildew, but this isn't apparent until colored washes are applied, when the patches of mildew come out in blotches. The painting surface is destroyed by anything that makes it less absorbent (such as oil spots), or more absorbent (like bruises).

Brushes. When storing brushes after use, wash them in lukewarm water and mild soap, as you would wash any other animal fiber such as wool. Strong soaps or too hot water remove the oil natural to the sable, ox or camel hair, so the hairs become brittle and break off. Rinse well and dry them thoroughly, for if stored damp, they may mildew. Seal them tightly with moth crystals. Brushes, like a sable coat, are made of fur and should have the same care.

If you are painting continuously, wash the brushes with soap and let them dry completely about once a month to remove the gummy substance that collects from the paint after prolonged use. If you can't spare the brushes long enough to let them dry for a couple of days, you may alternate between two sets.

Paint. To prevent your reserve supply of paint tubes from drying out, store them in tightly fitting screw-top jars, such as coffee jars.

To remoisten pigments that have gotten too hard, remove the cap and ram a nail or match stick down inside and fill the hole with water. Replace the cap and set aside for several days to allow the paint to absorb the moisture.

Some painters add water by opening the tubes at the bottom, and re-sealing by pinching with pliers; others "dunk" the unopened tubes in a jar of water for several months, or seal them in a jar containing a wet sponge, allowing the moisture to seep in slowly; but of course the labels come off.

Caps stick because paint has accumulated in the threads and dried. Soften the paint, either by dropping the tube into water for five or ten minutes or by heating the cap with a match. Once you have removed it, clean the threads with an old toothbrush.

Before each painting session make sure you have plenty of fresh, moist paint squeezed out so that you can pick it up on your brush easily, without digging and scrubbing. Add water to the dried pigment on your palette, preferably the night before, to give it a chance to absorb evenly.

To consolidate brushes. To save space in your paint box or brush holder, and to facilitate speed in reaching for a brush, you may wish to consolidate two brushes on one handle. Select the two which you use most often together. Remove the smaller of the two handles from its ferrule. Whittle down the end of the larger handle and fit the smaller ferrule onto it. The ferrule may be fastened to its new handle with cement or tape. Double-ended brushes like this cannot, of course, be carried vertically, or one end will be bent. Painters who make frequent use of a knife find it convenient to have the blade strapped to the end of their principal brush (as is shown in Plate 2).

Sponging paper. Manufacturers usually coat handmade paper with a sizing to protect the delicate surface from scratches in shipment. As the sizing varies in heaviness, in order to ensure even control of rough brushing and speed in laying on washes, it is best first to remove the sizing with a sponge or cloth and then to dry the paper flat on newspapers or thumbtacked to the wall. Since it will not be evident when dry which side has been treated, mark it, or better still, sponge both sides. Dampen only enough for immediate use, since without sizing the paper is vulnerable to scratches.

Oil spots may usually be detected before painting by sponging the paper and holding it up to the light.

To flatten paper which has buckled. Dampen the back of the painting and place a blotter or blanket next to the wet side, then press flat between weighted boards. Insert dry blotters and press again until dry, usually overnight.

To keep paper moist during painting. For techniques in which a great deal must be done in one drying period, the drying may be delayed by sponging both sides of the paper and painting with it on a wet pad made of soaked newspapers, blanket, or blotter, or by adding glycerine or glucose to the water (see Chapter XV on "Wet Blending").

To dry paper quickly. Place flat on a radiator or oven and dry both sides. If you put it inside the oven, leave the door open, turn the heat very low, and do not abandon it! An electric hair dryer is even better for speeding the drying time.

While this equipment and its care may be as good as any available today, each year, of course, will bring changes in the accoutrements of the painter.

P.F.

CHAPTER III

A WATERCOLOR PALETTE

EVERY PAINTER will discover through experience the palette or choice of pigments most useful to him. He will find, possibly, that he has more need for certain colors in the painting of one type of watercolor than of another. There is no set formula for the painting of portraits, because tastes vary. There is, however, a certain combination of pigments that may prove helpful to the beginner as a base from which he may mix the colors for nearly all skin tones, and on which he may build his own palette. The palette consists of:

Intense Colors

alizarin crimson
brilliant orange 1 (or alizarin orange)
brilliant yellow 2 (or cadmium yellow medium)
pthalocyanine green
pthalocyanine blue
ultramarine blue (or cobalt blue)

Neutrals

Mars violet (Mars red or Indian red)
burnt sienna
raw sienna
raw umber
Van Dyck brown

For flesh in direct light (under normal bright indoor lighting conditions) the combination of alizarin crimson and brilliant yellow 2 is recommended. These two colors are both vivid and must be painted in a very light wash.

In this way the painter takes advantage of the neutralizing effect of the white paper in order to avoid garish colors. Tore Asplund makes good use of this knowledge in his "Nude" (Plate 3). Since shadow is darker than light, and color in shadow is often more neutral than color in light, another neutralizing agent is required for the painting of shadow. It is suggested that Mars red (or Indian red) or Mars violet be mixed with the two more brilliant pigments, alizarin crimson and burnt sienna.

Of course, should the painter prefer, he may neutralize his brilliant colors by the use of their complements or black.

Saturated blue and green may be employed, but with caution, for, when mixed in the wrong proportion with certain warm colors, they will turn black or result in "muddy" or indeterminate color. The amount of each to be used is important. Experimenting with color mixing will prove a valuable exercise.

These two sets of colors are flexible and may be varied by any others the painter may favor. Neutral violet may be substituted for neutral red if a darker, cooler shadow is desired. If a shadow indoors is allowed to become too blue, it will advance rather than recede, because, under indoor lighting, shadows are often warm and highlights, cool.

For the painting of hair, the portrait palette may expand to include black. Black, if mixed with a small amount of burnt sienna or alizarin crimson to enliven it, makes a rich mixture for the deepest shadows in dark hair. Warning here should be offered against the indiscriminate use of black for skin tones. It is not taboo, when properly handled, but can very easily kill a shadow if mixed incorrectly.

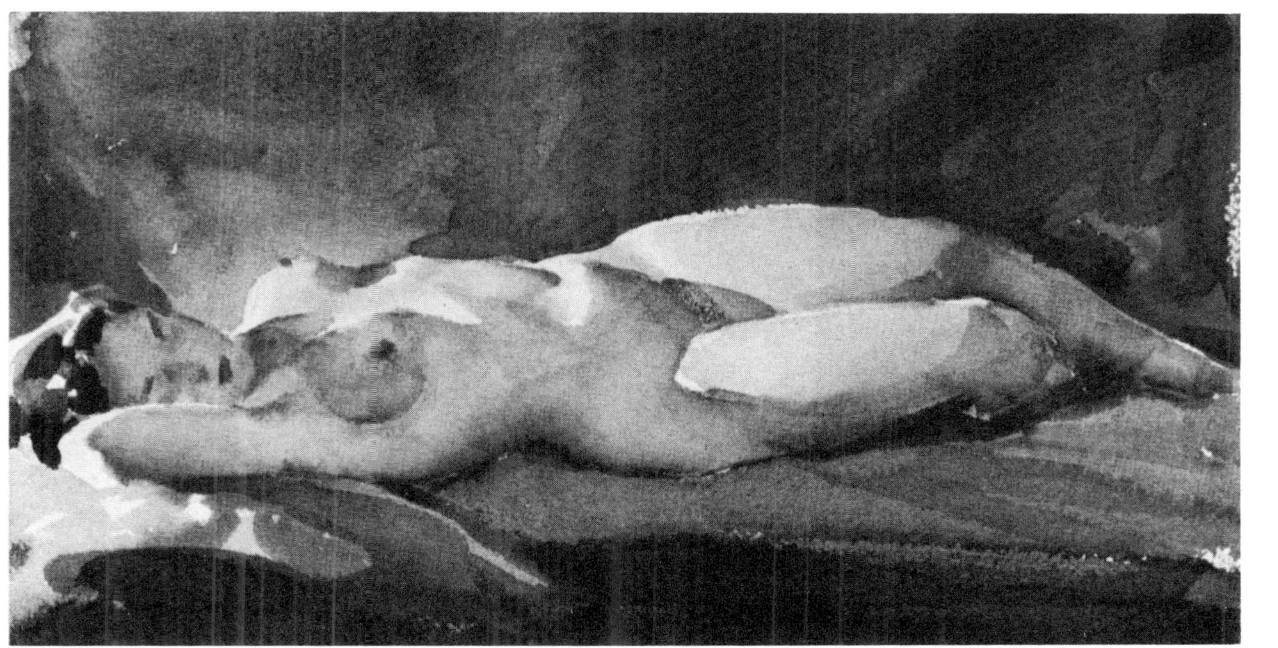

PLATE 3. Tore Asplund: "Nude." Like skin, watercolor is transparent. *Courtesy of Watson-Guptill Publications, Inc.*

A portrait palette may also contain a tube of Chinese white. This should be used only for the painting of accents, such as highlights in the eyes, and may never be mixed with another color, unless the portrait is to be painted entirely in gouache.

Each setup will require some variation from this suggested palette. The changes, of course, will depend on local lighting conditions and on what each artist sees. The foregoing suggestions may not apply when the artist wishes to distort a subject to achieve a mood, or otherwise intentionally departs from the realistic for a specific purpose.

For a further discussion of pigments, turn to the next chapter, which deals with "A Staining and Transparent Palette."

D.S.

CHAPTER IV

A STAINING AND TRANSPARENT PALETTE

by CARL N. SCHMALZ JR.

WATERCOLOR is essentially a transparent medium, and many of its most charming features are directly dependent on its transparency. This quality offers to the watercolor portraitist the opportunity for overpainting, a method long favored among tempera, fresco, and oil painters for obtaining that play of warm and cool color so necessary in flesh tones. The main objection to overpainting in watercolor always has been that, with the application of the second coat of paint, the first coat was either smeared or washed off. Some watercolors now on the market, however, greatly reduce this danger and make overpainting practicable. This chapter explains how to recognize these paints and how to create a transparent and staining palette.

All artists' paint is a mixture of binder and coloring matter. In watercolor the binder is composed mainly of gum arabic and glycerine, but coloring matter is either pigment or dye, the pigment paints being by far the more numerous.

In a pigment paint, small particles of coloring matter are suspended in the binder. The size of these particles varies with the different pigments. Cobalt blue, for example, must be left in relatively large fragments in order to preserve its brilliance, but cadmium yellow is most satisfactory when ground extremely fine. When any pigment color is applied as paint, the medium—water—evaporates, leaving a layer of tiny particles distributed over the surface of the paper and held in place by the binder. Thus, lines or colors underneath a coat of pigment paint will be wholly or partially obscured. Also, since the binder is readily soluble in water, even after thorough drying the thin layers of particles can be loosened and easily washed off. The more finely ground pigments, of course, tend to settle into the pores of the paper and for that reason are usually more difficult to wash off than the coarser ones. As pigment particles tend, also, to lodge in the depressions of rough paper, smooth paper can be washed cleaner. Finally, since the transparency of a pigment depends more on its power to bend light rays than on the size of its particles, the finely ground colors like the cadmiums will, in some cases, be more opaque than cobalt blue and other coarse pigments.

The paints made with dyes consist of chemical compounds in direct solution in the binder instead of being particles of coloring matter in suspension. They are completely transparent because they leave no paint grains on the surface of the paper, but flow with the water down into its pores, staining the fibers. Most dyes, however, are more easily made into paint if they can be united with a chemically inert substance like alumina hydrate or chalk. These paints are called "lakes," and though not quite so transparent as the pure dyes, act like them in that they stain the paper. For this reason, dye colors, whether they are pure or lakes, are almost impossible to remove.

Thus, the composition of a watercolor paint directly influences its degree of staining power and transparency.

Colors are usually transparent in about the same proportion as they are stainers. That is, the most transparent colors are the dyes, which are also the most penetrating, and by the same token, the most opaque pigments are generally the most easily washed off. Since the staining colors, necessary in underpainting, are at the same time transparent colors, which are useful in overpainting, the same palette may be used for both functions.

Paints put up by different manufacturers under the same name frequently vary in composition as well as hue, and they are rarely labeled exactly. Since this is particularly true in regard to the student grades, it is valuable for the practicing artist to be able to test his own colors when making up a transparent and staining palette. The following two simple tests are recommended:

1. *To test staining power:* paint strips of the colors you wish to try on a fresh piece of good rag paper. When they are completely dry, cut the paper so that half the strip is left; then wash off the other half with warm water and a brush. By comparing it with the original, it is possible to see just how much of the paint remains. As predicted, the dyes will be least altered and the coarse pigments most faded. Under such violent treatment, of course, some of the color comes off no matter what type of paint is used.

2. *To test transparency:* lay a heavy strip of black paint on a sheet of clean paper. When it is thoroughly dry, brush narrow strokes of each paint to be tested across the black. The very opaque pigments, like the cadmiums, will show clearly on the black when dry, but little trace of the dye colors will be visible where they overlie the black

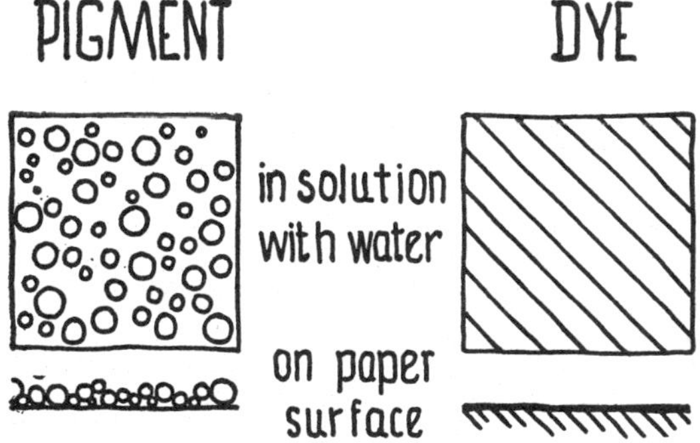

Fig. 1: Pigments and Dyes

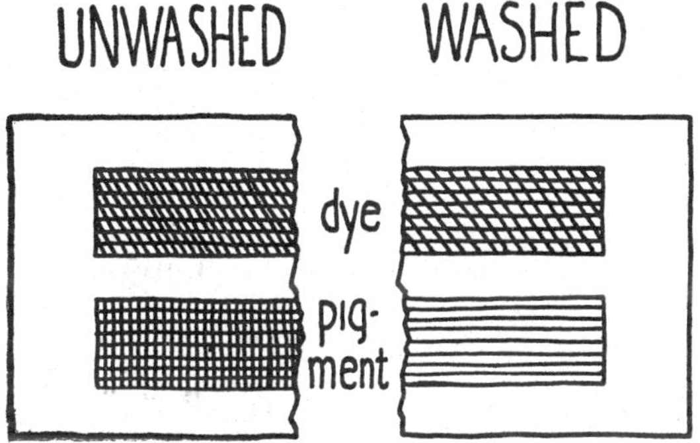

Fig. 2: Unwashed and Washed Paints

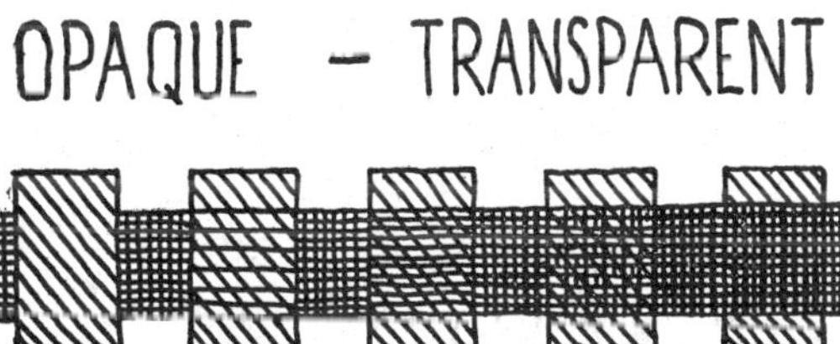

Fig. 3: Opaque and Transparent Colors

PLATE 4. Carl N. Schmalz Jr. Three Diagrams

strip. This method was devised by James M. Pace, a student at the O'Hara Watercolor School.

During the summer of 1946, I submitted all the colors available at the O'Hara School to the two tests just described. These included permanent paints manufactured by several different companies. The final results of my investigation suggested that there are very few transparent or staining colors on the market today. The paints ranking highest on both tests were the pthalocyanine dye colors, green and blue, and alizarin crimson, a synthetic lake. In order to complete a staining and transparent palette, a yellow, a warm red, and a true blue were needed. Tests indicated that Indian yellow was the most transparent and most penetrating of the true yellows. The paint that today is called Indian yellow is generally either a synthetic pigment or a lake color made from the Hansa dye group, and is at least as permanent as alizarin crimson. I used it, therefore, in mixtures with alizarin for my orange and vermilion hues. Further experimentation showed that pthalocyanine blue mixed with alizarin crimson will produce an ultramarine or a cobalt substitute, depending on the ratio of the mixers. These mixtures, of course, are somewhat neutralized, but in flesh painting brilliant blues are rarely necessary.

Hence, alizarin crimson, pthalocyanine blue and green, and Indian yellow yield a workable basic palette of staining and transparent colors.

A comparatively fine-grained pigment like lamp black may serve fairly well as a neutral, though I have found that a mixture of alizarin and pthalocyanine green produces a livelier and more transparent dark. A complete black is not often necessary in skin tones, but the alizarin crimson–pthalocyanine green mixture will be found very useful in combination with the brilliant colors. The imaginative artist will find infinite ways of varying his mixtures in order to produce other hues suitable to his needs.

These conclusions may be conveniently summarized in the following palette:

Hue	*Tube Colors*	*Mixed Colors*
bluish red	alizarin crimson	
blue		pthalocyanine blue and alizarin crimson
greenish blue	pthalocyanine blue	
bluish green	pthalocyanine green	
green		pthalocyanine green and Indian yellow
yellow	Indian yellow	
orange		Indian yellow and alizarin crimson
red-orange		alizarin crimson and Indian yellow
red		alizarin crimson and less Indian yellow
neutral		alizarin crimson and pthalocyanine green

The artist who wishes to simplify his palette to three tube colors may dispense with pthalocyanine green and substitute pthalocyanine blue mixed with yellow. With these three colors it is also possible to mix, not only a yellow orange, but also neutrals comparable to burnt sienna, sepia, Van Dyck brown, or raw umber; or better still, to neutralize exact spectrum hues: neutral red, neutral orange, neutral yellow, and so forth.

By underpainting with staining colors, the watercolorist may reduce the danger of smearing so as to proceed in comparative safety. For the overpainted coats, of course, the use of stainers is not so necessary, since these colors do not have to withstand the repeated flooding of new washes. Being transparent, however, the staining palette is useful also in overpainting, though some more opaque areas are usually desirable in the finished picture.

Through the use of these simple tests of transparency and staining power, the watercolorist can determine fairly accurately which of his paints are best suited for underpainting, and which for overpainting. With this information he should be able to take advantage of one more of the characteristics peculiar to his medium.

NOTE (1985)

The basic information and procedures described in this chapter remain useful, but a more recent and fuller explanation of pigment properties will be found in "Transparent and Opaque," Chapter 10 in my *Watercolor Your Way* (Watson-Guptill, 1978). For transparency testing, black waterproof ink may be substituted for black watercolor paint. What is here called Indian yellow is often called Hansa yellow today. Also, the new transparent pigments in the purple/violet range should be included in the list of available colors for a staining and transparent palette, and sap green, phthalocyanine blue, and alizarin crimson may be mixed to produce a staining terre verte.

Gettens, R. J., and G. L. Stout. *Painting Materials, a Short Encyclopaedia.* New York: D. Van Nostrand Co., Inc., 1942. (Dover reprint)

Kay, Reed. *Painter's Guide to Studio Methods and Materials.* Englewood Cliffs, NJ: Prentice-Hall, 1982.

Mayer, Ralph. *The Artist's Handbook of Materials and Techniques.* 3rd edition. New York: The Viking Press, 1970.

CHAPTER V

DISTRIBUTION OF ELEMENTS

NOW THAT some of the fundamentals for watercolor portraiture have been considered, the student is ready to select a subject and commit his ideas to paper. What should be his first concern?

Early in his study he should begin to visualize the design of his picture, even if he spends only a few minutes at the start of each drawing in consideration of the size and location of the all important head and the other contributing elements. Neglect of design at this stage may bring on "bull's-eye-itis" (a complaint common among art students). Once infected, he goes on depositing a face like an ace of spades in the middle of his canvas or paper, or he may place it always slightly above the center.

In point of fact many of our contemporary portraitists might do well to take an occasional hint from the photographers they have been selling short for the last twenty years. A portrait in the medium of photography can be just as well spotted as a painted head, and camera artists like Robert Krasker, Laura Gilpin, or the late Alfred Stieglitz, in some of their portraits or closeups, use infinitely more interesting placement than many of the men and women now rendering heads in oil.

Piet Mondrian, we are told, used to prepare a smooth white panel and then with heavy black lines cut it up into rectangles. The rectangles, usually placed either horizontally or vertically, avoid a dynamic quality such as might result from diagonals. If a design like this escapes being static, any feeling of motion must result from variations in the size and position of areas and the fact that one or two of these segments may become accents by filling them in with black or a color.

We must be severe self-disciplinarians if we are to experiment, as did Mondrian, with quantity isolated from the less basic conceptions such as direction, form, value, color, and texture. Even our division lines should not vary in size, for shading implies quality rather than quantity. In your experiments use rectangles of all different dimensions.

The resulting arrangements will be desirable or not by virtue of their spotting or placement alone. You will like them or not just as you prefer one person to another, often without being able to assign a reason. In such subjective painting, and even when you have left the realm of pure design and are planning a portrait, your feelings are always a safer criterion than any set of rules or adaptation of compositions used by successful painters.

It is noticeable, however, that very few great pictures contain uniform areas. Uccello, Gauguin, and Matisse, as well as other decorative artists, have an instinct for balance and use interesting sequence in areas. Although achieving original juxtapositions, they seldom repeat spacing unless for purposes of rhythm or contrast.

Having experimented in rectangular divisions of a light-colored ground by dark lines, try a series with an elliptical spot for the face and smaller ones for a hand or an item of dress. Judge these on grounds of dimension, quantity, and placement, as you did the rectangles. If this spot for the face always occupies the same position on the

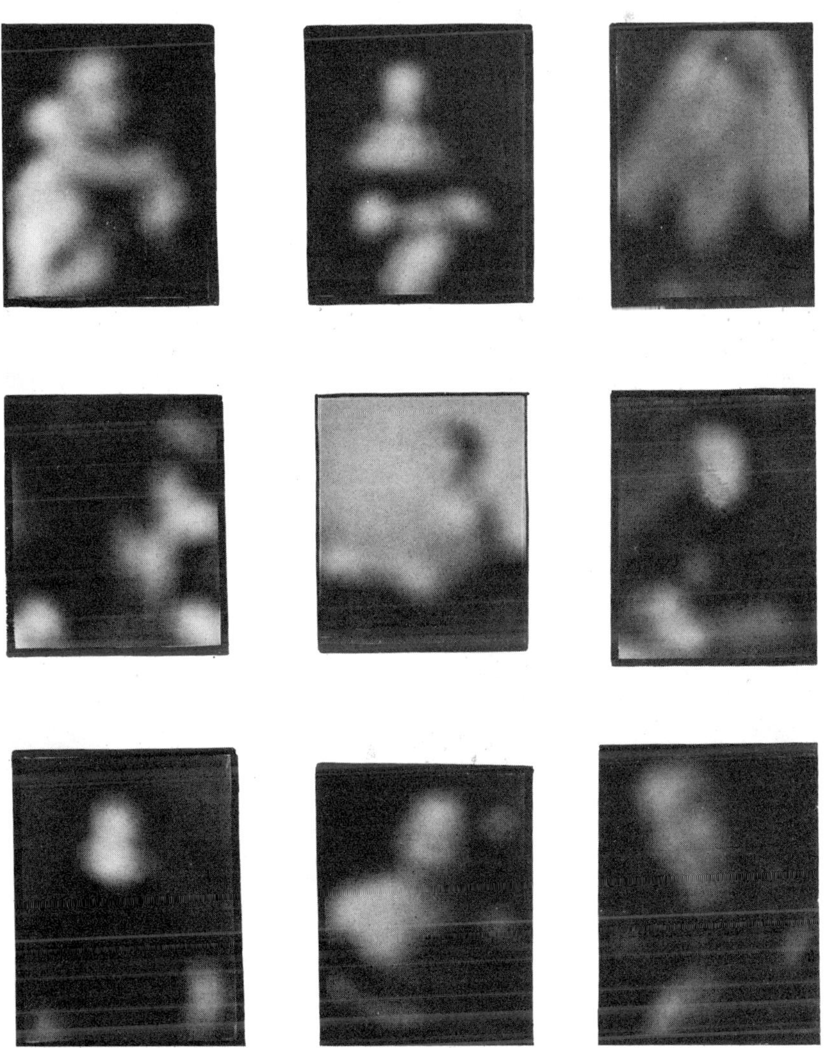

PLATE 5. Nine Masterpieces Diffused to Show "Spotting" in the Distribution of Elements.

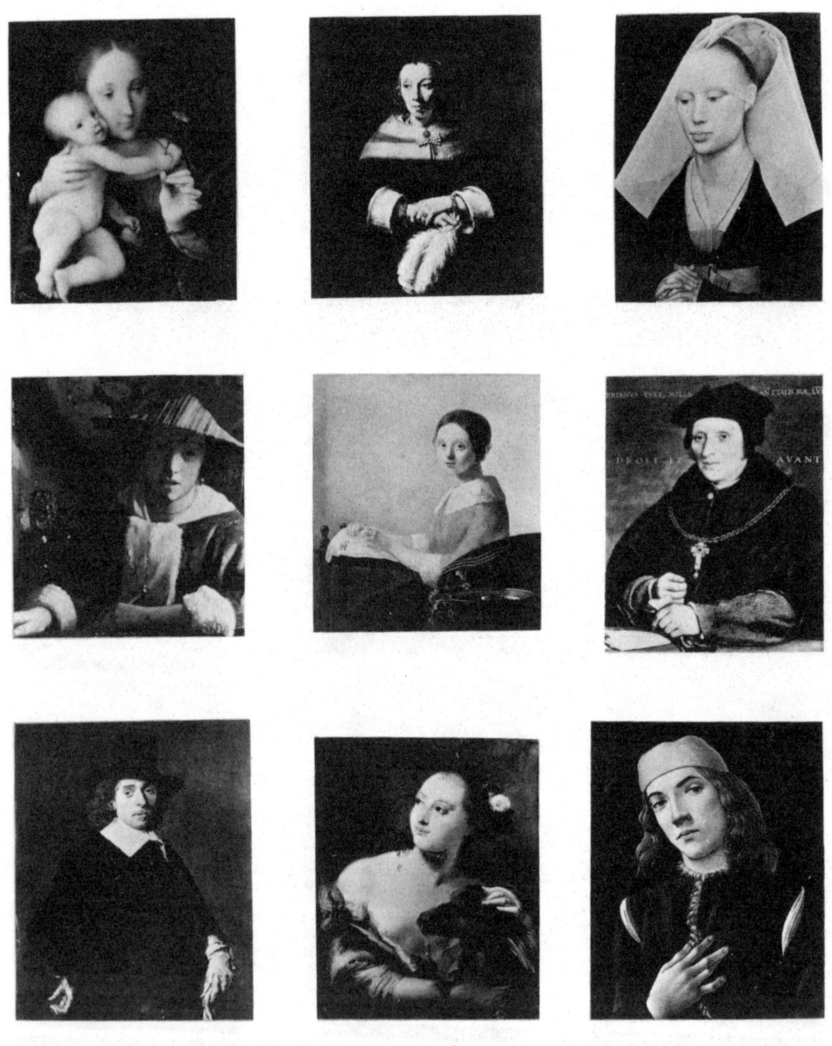

PLATE 6.

Key to Illustrations for "Spotting"
Nine Masterpieces from the National Gallery of Art, Washington, D. C.

"Madonna and Child" (oil)
by Correggio (?)
(*Kress Collection*)

"Portrait of a Lady with an Ostrich-Feather Fan" (oil)
by Rembrandt van Ryn
(*Widener Collection*)

"Portrait of a Lady (tempera and oil)
by Rogier van der Weyden
(*Mellon Collection*)

"A Young Girl with a Flute" (oil)
by Jan Vermeer
(*Widener Collection*)

"The Lacemaker" (oil)
by Jan Vermeer
(*Mellon Collection*)

"Sir Brian Tuke" (tempera and oil)
by Hans Holbein the Younger
(*Mellon Collection*)

"Portrait of a Man" (oil)
by Frans Hals
(*Widener Collection*)

"A Young Woman with a Parrot" (pastel)
by Giovanni Battista Tiepolo
(*Kress Collection*)

"Portrait of a Youth" (tempera and oil)
by Sandro Botticelli
(*Mellon Collection*)

canvas, that is monotony and as such is resented, although perhaps unconsciously, by the observer.

Plates 5 and 6 show two photographs, one out of focus, one in, of a group of nine different spottings for portraits. If the page as a whole seems monotonous the fault is my own, since I wished to show variations within the kind of rectangle most traditional with portrait painters. The variety in size and distribution of the spots is attributable to nine masters of the past.

Now try a third series of abstract positions on a paper; this time in three values, light, dark, and middle tone. Take them from some chance victim sitting in the room with you. How would you frame her if that was your intention, and in what variety of positions and proportions could she gaze down at you from the wall?

Compare these trials and ask yourself which setup is best from the point of view of design as pattern on a canvas or paper. Remember that our task is threefold: the portrait should be good in arrangement as well as in resemblance to the sitter and should also interpret his character.

Make a few of these little "thumbnail" sketches before starting each picture. The fact that your work for the day happens to be a study rather than a commissioned portrait is no excuse at all for depositing the unhappy subject's face right in the center of a vast sheet of paper. At the turn of the century, estimable ladies treated pots of zinnias to this ignominy. One thoughtful art teacher found a remedy, after he realized that this practice of unconsciously centering any subject might start with elementary work on casts and life models. In his classes he required that his beginners arrange their cast hands, ears, horses' heads, etc., in a composition, and rated the results as much on plan as on drawing.

A good football coach never allows a ball to roll about on the ground, and he reprimands any member of the squad who doesn't "fall on it." The coach wants it to be second nature to secure any fumble immediately. In the same way, any exercise on paper, no matter how trivial it may seem, should be conceived as a design. A little thought at the time of starting a drawing will guard you against dull compositions later.

E.O'H.

CHAPTER VI

MODELING WITH PAINT

PART I

WATERCOLOR IS NOT a fortunate medium for the painter who is tentative by temperament. An exception, of course, is he who is using it not to become a portrait painter but as occupational therapy to help him make other decisions quickly. It certainly leaves no time for alternatives and minor self-questionings.

Since in watercolor it is more difficult than in any of the opaque mediums to paint out mistakes and correct errors of value and outline, more preliminary training is desirable before one attempts the actual portrait.

In these exercises always use white paper, preferably rough, and black paint. The paper should be sponged and dried beforehand to remove sizing and oily finger marks.

This is a critical stage for the one who would master transparent watercolor, since, while there are many ways of doctoring up irregularities in a smooth wash and many tricks for covering up mistakes, it is best to have no crutches to lean on until you have learned to get along without them. Double painting, rough brushing, and "whisking" strokes, used both as direct technique and in repair procedures, will be taken up later, in Chapters IX, XI, and XXI.

Suppose that you now paint a cylinder about five inches

in diameter (see Plate 7). As the highlight only rarely has a hard outline, the transition can be eased by blending it from pure water into color. Do this with paint corresponding to the value of the local color on the light side. Hold the paper so that you may see, by the reflection from a skylight or window, that it is evenly wet. The extra water that drains to the lower edge can be blotted off. When the paper is uniformly damp, charge the brush with more paint, enough to make the darkest value desired. Make allowance for the fact that watercolor always dries lighter than it appears when wet. Do not let the brush be wetter than the paper. Since it is evenly wet, any extra water will merely dilute the paint and make it run. At each step in the drying, the brush, also, should contain less moisture. Too dry a brush, on the other hand, will remove most of the color.

With this evenly charged brush then paint a straight band on the darkest part of the shadow side. Stroke in only one direction and be sure that the brush is full of paint right up to the metal ferrule. Another way is to scumble around the highlight when first wetting the surface.

The area of the cylinder now consists of a highlight either blended from pure water or scumbled into the value of the lighted side. On this you have put a band of black with hard edges. All is evenly wet (see no. 1, Plate 7).

Clean the brush in water and shape it by squeezing it between the thumb and forefinger or by stroking it across the jar's rim, then on a rag laid flat on your table. Stroke with it held vertically and with only the tip touching the paper. The one-inch brush should overlap the stripe half way. Make one even stroke only, then move the brush slightly toward the light and stroke again. You may wish to stroke for a third time slightly back toward the dark. This should make an even blend away from one side of the black stripe by carrying some of the paint from the band itself toward the light. What the brush should now do is redistribute the paint already on the paper, spreading it evenly and making it grade from light to dark (no. 2, Plate 7).

When working in color, there is almost always a difference in hue between the shadow and the reflected light, and were the reflected light to be painted merely a paler value of the shadow color, the portrait would become a monochrome. After the shadow, therefore, the brush must be rinsed and recharged for the reflected light, easing the transition into the shadow.

The procedure for another geometric shape, the dome, is like that for the cylinder, except that the highlight, instead of being a straight line, may be curved or crescent shaped. The darkest area too will vary in shape from straightness.

In all of this work the brush should not stop in the middle of an area, for that would leave a light spot. A light whisking stroke is best, too, because bearing down hard bends the hairs and paint cannot flow as readily onto the surface.

Since rough paper has more grain to hold wetness and dries less quickly than smooth, use the former, at least in the beginning.

In practicing, now try cylinders and domes that will have the highlight and shadows in various positions and be illuminated differently.

Another way of making a cylinder is to do it all by scumbling or rough brushing. As rough brushing will be fully described later in a separate chapter, for the present use mostly blended washes.

You will find that if the brush moves sideways and flat, the hairs will lift paint off the paper, whereas a vertically held brush puts paint on. Be sure that the reflected light in shadow is darker than the light side of the cylinder. As long as the surface is damp it can be modeled, but the moment that any portion is almost dry one should stop work entirely, for the wet brush will double paint the dry parts and dilute the still damp section.

Since not one out of a hundred beginners in watercolor will be able at once to accomplish these cylinders and domes, we feel that a more detailed approach will be helpful and not seem too repetitious. Walter B. Colebrook, an instructor at the O'Hara School and the Norton School of Art, will suggest further exercises for this method of training.

PART II

Although there are many problems of technique to solve in each watercolor portrait, improvement in one's skill eliminates excessive concern over this major hurdle. The best way to attain facility is through practice with a systematic series of exercises in which the handling of paint is the only consideration.

We shall deal with difficulties peculiar to watercolor portrait painting, roughly in the order in which they are encountered.

The brush that has proved most useful for the broad treatment that gives watercolor its characteristic freshness is a one-inch flat-stroke with three-quarter-inch hairs (red sable), although the regular one-inch flat-stroke is equally satisfactory. For this series of exercises, use either lamp black or ivory black and any good rough watercolor paper.

The first consideration in modeling in watercolor is transition. This may be in value (from dark to light), in hue (red-orange to yellow, for example), in intensity (from a brilliant to a more neutralized hue), or in combinations of these.

EXERCISE NO. 1

The exercises begin with the setting down in pencil of a four-inch square. Indicate with a pencil where you plan to have middle and light values. This marking beforehand toward a predetermined goal is advisable in all these exercises, since we are striving for a control of the medium. (This will be a simple transition, not a cylinder.) Wet this area with clean water; glance along its surface to be certain that it is completely and evenly dampened. The surface of the paper and the brush must be equally wet, since a wetter brush leaves puddles of water, and a too dry brush will remove moisture. Now, without adding more water, fully load the brush with a rich value of the black, and paint evenly down the dark half of the wet area. Wash the brush, and squeeze it out until it again matches the paper in moisture.

Begin at the top, straddling the division between the painted and the merely dampened areas, and move with a light but steady stroke to the bottom. Without rinsing the brush make another stroke a quarter of an inch farther into the unpainted half. The third stroke should begin a quarter of an inch farther into the dark side than the first blending stroke, and again move to the lower edge. This has the effect of producing six stripes of graded value, each of which, being of the same wetness as its adjoining stripe, fuses with it, giving an even blend from the dark to the light. Starting them at different points (no. 1, Plate 7) discloses the effect of these strokes, although the starting point of the last one is not visible. Repeat this exercise until you get a smooth transition of a predetermined pattern. This is the foundation of good watercolor technique.

A variation useful for making transitions over larger areas, or when using a smaller brush, is the practice of painting in the local color or value, working into the highlight area, then quickly adding the dark portion, which is thus blended into the still wet local color or value.

For very small transitions such as frequently occur at the corner of the mouth, the edge of the nostril, on the bone over the eye socket, etc. (Plate 7), a stroke of dark paint may be softened on one side by immediately rinsing the brush and stroking one edge of the line with clear water, allowing the paint to flow gradually away from the hard edge.

EXERCISE NO. 2

This exercise consists of making a second square. This time have it light in the center and dark on both sides. The blending is done by the same method as before—that of uniformly wetting the entire surface, then adding the darkest areas, and, while they are still wet, blending the stripes. By overlapping single strokes the brush can be made to carry paint from the dark into the light.

Since you have cleaned the brush, and then picked up paint by stroking the dark strip "half on and half off," the brush is now double charged. As you blend alternate sides of an area, turn the brush over to avoid a hard edge.

After a few times you will attain the faster working pace needed to do transitions within the drying time. Then wipe out a reflected light along the dark edge with a clean, fairly dry brush held flat.

EXERCISE NO. 3

Matching an already dry transition is the third exercise (no. 3, Plate 7). Set down the first small area, perhaps wo by four inches. Let this get bone dry. Directly under it make a second area of the same size. Duplicate the first in value and in rate of change from light to dark. Remember—all areas appear darker while wet than they will after drying. As Mr. O'Hara says, "If it looks right, it's wrong. Make it darker."

EXERCISE NO. 4

The fourth exercise is on splicing adjoining areas without leaving hard edges. Since this series of exercises is cumulative, the last is an application of the foregoing three.

Set down an area of about three by four inches. Start with any value, preferably a dark one, and make a gradual transition to white paper (no. 4, Plate 7). Allow this to get completely dry. (Working into a partly dry area is fatal to good results.) Gently rewet with clean water, without going back over it a second time. Begin painting at the white paper side with a value to match the dark end of the area. Make the transition in the opposite direction, decreasing the amount of color in the second wash as it approaches the dark part of the first. This superimposed coat should give an even value over the entire area with no signs of double-painted or hard-edged joining.

WALTER B. COLEBROOK

Having practiced all of these exercises directed toward painting merely to show form, you may extend the lesson to modeling heads of actual people. Try treating them as simple egglike forms with cylinders for the neck. Each head is different in proportions and basic shape; the dome

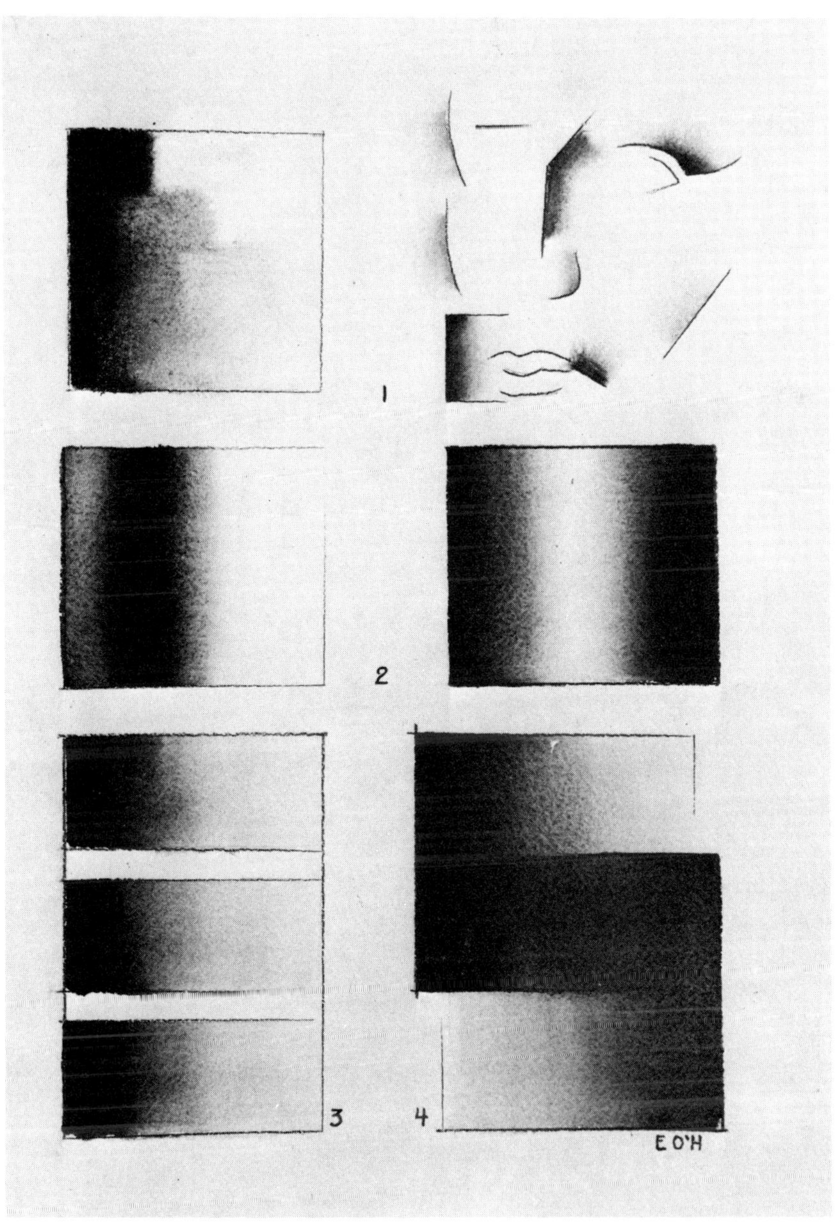

PLATE 7. Eliot O'Hara: Modeling with Paint. The tackling dummies for training in technique.

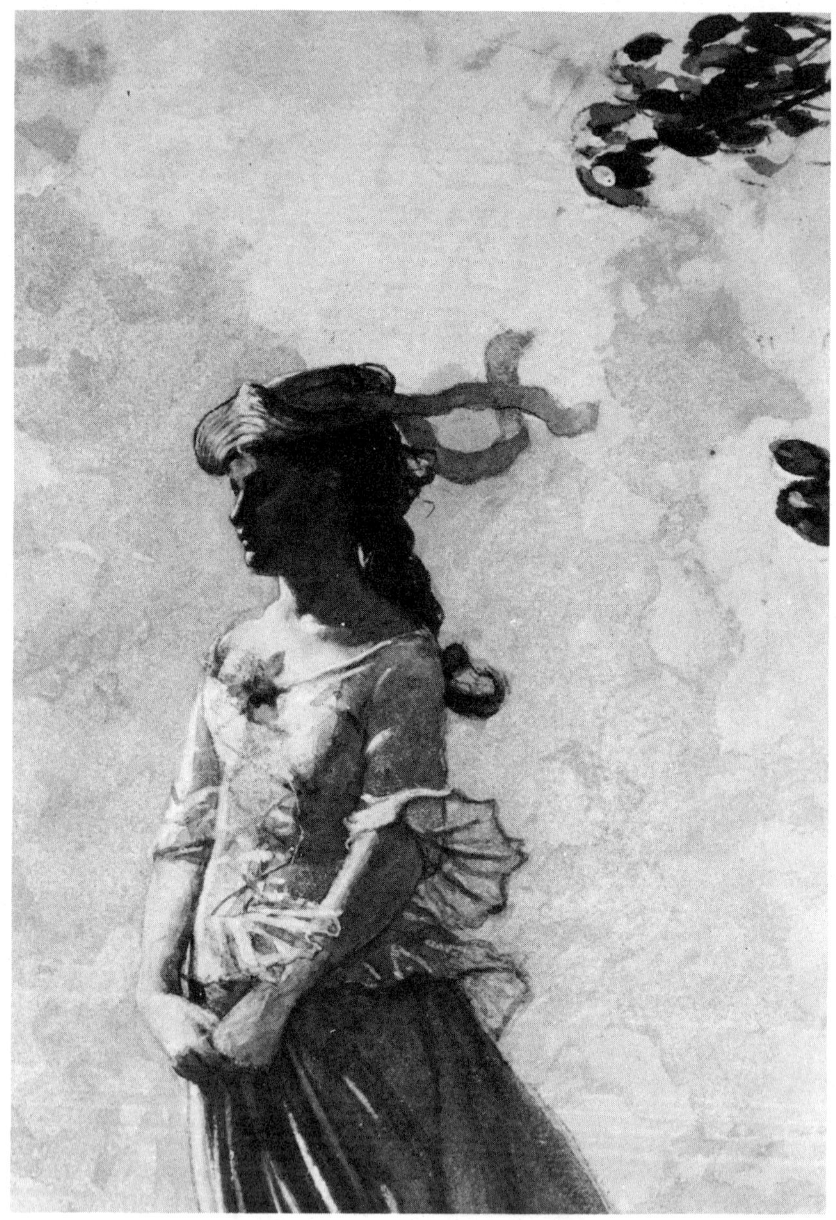

PLATE 8. Winslow Homer: "Shepherdess"—detail. Nature and circumstances often provide a ready-made setup. *In the Brooklyn Museum Collection.*

of the skull may be round, conical, or squarish; and the mask of the face triangular, square, or round, wide or long; while the relationship between dome, mask, and neck is always different as concerns size, angles, and proportion.

Now try these same exercises in a variety of flesh colors to correspond to different complexions and colorings.

You don't have to persuade your family and neighbors to pose for you to get this observation practice in combined technique and basic form. In fact you will do better if you catch your subjects on the wing. As they move about you see them from various angles and conceive them as "in thc round" and without features.

Although we have been concerned here more with brush work than with building a likeness, we shall later tackle that problem. Before attempting a likeness, however, let us consider the pose, the lighting, and the rest of the miscellany referred to by artists as the "setup."

E.O'H.

CHAPTER VII

THE SETUP

THE COMPACT equipment of the watercolorist enables him to paint a portrait wherever there is favorable light and sufficient elbowroom. He need not be impeded by the easels, model stands, fancy work tables, numerous bottles and jars, and dozens of brushes, which confine to his studio the painter in a more cumbersome medium.

This easy portability ensures the watercolorist the maximum variety of settings for his portraits, which he will do well to make use of in planning his designs in order to bring out his sitters' personalities. Each time the artist goes to a different subject's home, he finds new background arrangements or lighting. Many artists prefer to work in their own studios, where they are familiar with the conditions and lighting possibilities and are in control of interruptions and possible distractions.

Because portrait painting is usually done indoors, it is concerned with light originating from specific sources. Through control of its quantity and direction the painter achieves the best interpretation of his subject.

Direct light falls on the portion of the spherical form of the head that is nearest the source of illumination, but where the surfaces turn away, the areas are cast into deep shadow which may be lessened by a secondary illumination usually caused by light rays striking other objects and being deflected into the shadow. Cast shadow is the result of rays being blocked off by an intervening object.

Indoors, when the source is a reflection of the blue sky, highlights are cool and the adjacent lighted areas are warmed only by local color. Shadows are normally warm unless influenced by unusually blue or green surroundings. In the absence of natural illumination, lamps may be substituted. Since tungsten bulbs are yellow and artificial daylight bulbs blue, a combination of the two in a triple socket—in the proportion of one tungsten to two daylight—is recommended. Certain fluorescent tubes—soft white, 3500 white, 4500 white, and daylight—may serve as well. The painter would profit by experimentation with lights on the model for the purpose of distortion, but the paper and palette should be illuminated by light approximating that of day.

A secondary light, weaker in voltage or placed at a greater distance, or a pale reflector (which may be intentionally erected or may accidentally result from direct illumination on a portion of the setup) will relieve a too dense shadow.

Out of doors the direct rays from the sun bathe the object in a warm light. This causes shaded surfaces to be cool when they face the sky, and warm only when affected by a warm reflector. Especially at midday, sunlight will cause hard shadows that may tend to distort. The illusion of brilliant sunlight is achieved largely by contrasting the sunlit areas with the extreme darkness of adjacent shadows, as may be seen in the detail of Winslow Homer's "Shepherdess" (Plate 8), and by the strong light reflecting elsewhere into the shadows (as on the cheekbone, neck, arm, and skirt of the shepherdess).

Painters and photographers are particularly interested in utilizing light patterns to portray mood and personality. They often prefer front diffused lighting for soft, feminine, and youthful subjects, and cross lighting, which emphasizes texture and planes, for subjects of more vigorous character. Dramatic effects may be achieved by the unaccustomed illumination from beneath or behind, or the contour of a face brought out by that from the side. If placed too close, lights have a tendency to flatten a surface. To emphasize a mood further, it is useful to supply additional sources of light to point up certain salient features.

For a convincing natural effect, the background and subject should be affected by the same kind and direction of light. Likewise, a portrait should be completed under constant conditions in order to be consistent. It should, moreover, not be sold unless it looks well in the artificial light usual in a home where it might be hung.

The foregoing suggestions have dealt with a natural effect. They are not unbreakable rules, however, and may serve as a base from which one may distort for the sake of mood, as was done by David Fredenthal in "Stolen Bread" (Plate 10), where the surroundings, pose, and organization all contribute to a sense of squalor.

The side lighting of a home, which is often more becoming to the sitter than an overhead skylight or studio fixture, is also an advantage to the watercolorist. During most of the painting his board must be almost horizontal. An overhead light will shine directly on the paper, which, as soon as it is wet, will reflect such a glare that he is unable to see either the underlying drawing or the colors he is applying.

In selecting the room for the sitting, not only should the artist place himself far enough from the subject to reduce the effects of exaggerated foreshortening, but he

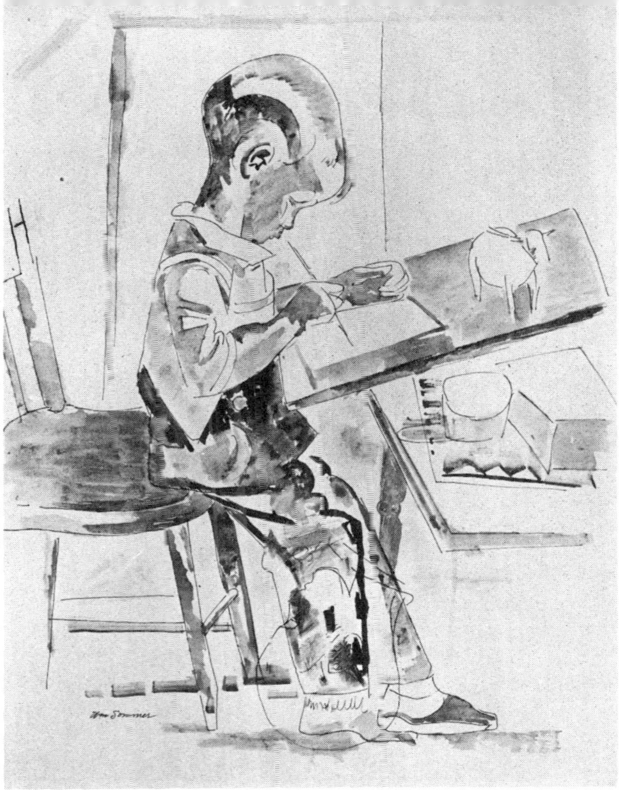

PLATE 9. William Sommer: "The First Lesson" (watercolor and ink). A delicate painting need not be weak. *Courtesy, Arno O. Bohme, Cleveland.*

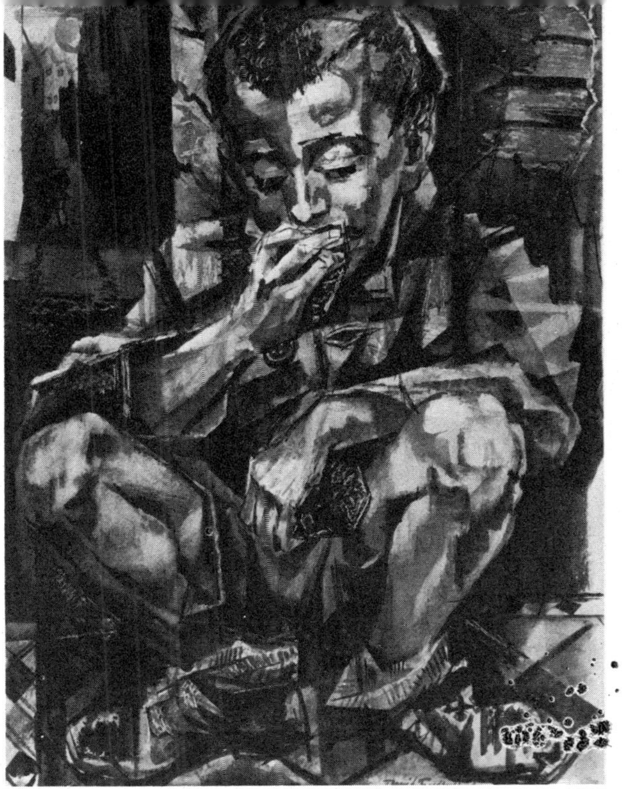

PLATE 10. David Fredenthal: "Stolen Bread." Here, in depth and strength, watercolor proves its versatility. *Courtesy, Charles H. Muhlenberg, Jr., Reading, Pa.*

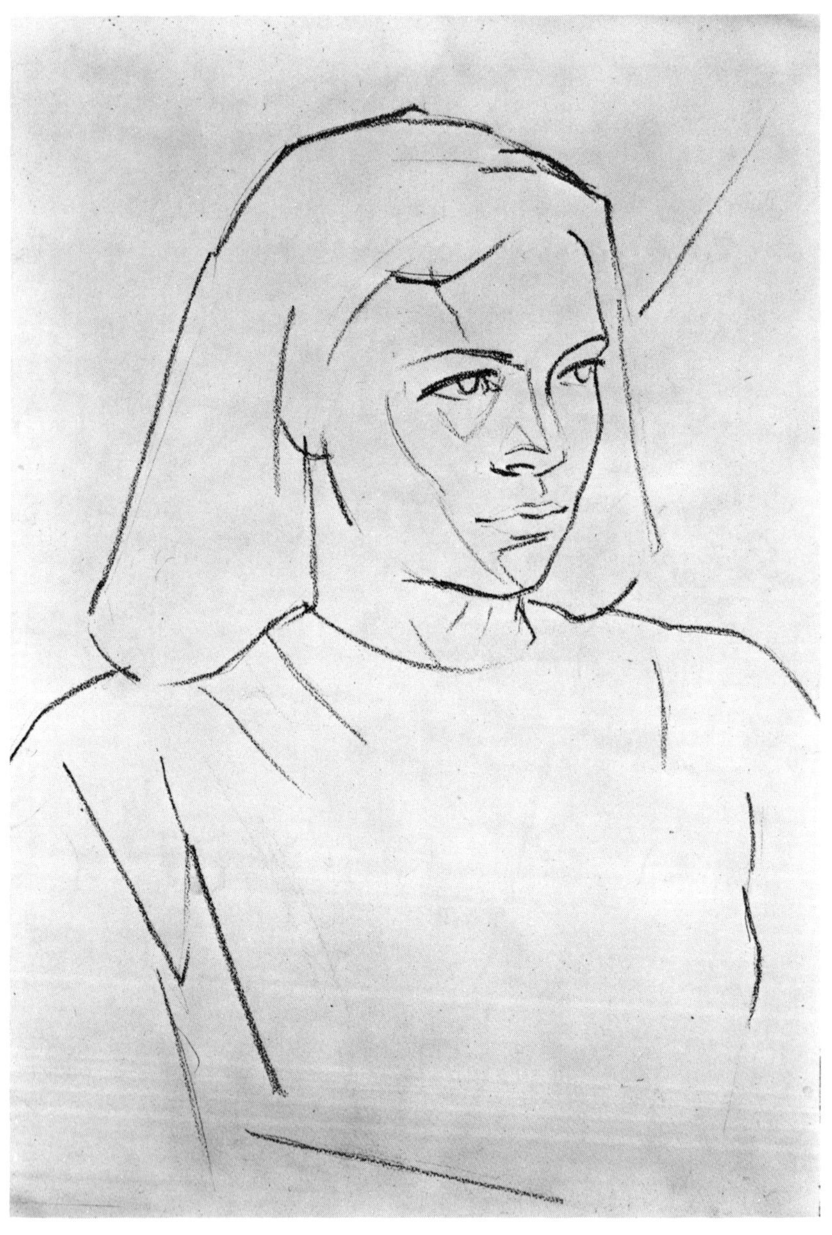

PLATE 11. Dorothy Short: The Drawing for "Toni in Yellow." The scaffolding can be constructed with either pencil or brush.

should also allow enough runway behind himself so that he can stand back to view both the model and the picture —a runway unencumbered with hazardous lamps and coffee tables.

While the painter is deciding on the lighting most suitable to his subject or, later, arranging his own materials, he should at the same time be watching for the most interesting pose. A standing position will necessitate more frequent rests, or, in some cases, may be eased by a table to sit or lean on. For a seated pose, the model himself should select the most comfortable chair. Often an absorbing activity on the part of the subject will present a more interesting picture than a more formal pose, as is demonstrated in "The First Lesson" by William Sommer (Plate 9), and in "Listening" (Plate 28) by Phoebe Flory.

The artist's position depends on the view he wishes to have of his subject and on his own working convenience.

Large groups or classes, of course, are seldom permitted all this latitude in settings, lighting, and posing of the model, which are necessarily averaged down to a few positions in the interest of giving everyone a good view. You might not need a model stand if the painters in the front row sit on low stools with their watercolors on the floor, and look up at the sitter. The middle group, seated, may arrange their equipment on benches or chairs and have an eye-level view. Those who stand at the back of the room may work at tables, since distance diminishes the foreshortening effects of looking down on the subject.

When the model is first engaged, whether paid to pose or invited for a private sitting, he should be told what is expected of him: that he will not be required to buy the portrait; how long the sitting will take; and whether you will need him for more than one session. For commissions, allowances should be made for a second sitting, in case the first portrait does not suit the buyer or the artist.

As soon as the pose is decided upon, you should mark with chalk on the floor the location of the chair or table the subject is using and outline his feet; and to help him to regain the pose, ask him to select a point straight in front of his head to which he may refer. He need not hold the position rigidly. If you quickly sketch in the action of the figure as you plan the composition and if, as you record the angle of the head, you include the horizontal and vertical perspective lines, you may permit him considerable latitude during the remainder of the sitting.

Tell him that the only thing that is *not* helpful to you is for him to freeze into a rigid pose. It would be better, therefore, if he talked and indulged in the minor movements of expression and conversation.

Although professional models are used to posing for twenty-five minutes out of each half hour, the amateur should seldom be required to pose more than twenty minutes, with at least ten-minute rests. When, however, a large wash must be completed in one drying time, warn him that you may ask him to pose a little longer.

When the direction of his gaze has been determined, tell him that you will ask him to look there for a few minutes only when you are working on the eyes, and at all other times he should be free to look at you or anywhere he wishes. A fixed gaze will not only make his eyes water, but will give an unpleasant stare to the portrait.

Since, when the mouth has been closed for some time, it is apt to droop at the corners or acquire a set expression, it should be painted immediately after a rest or while the model is talking, or when he thinks that you are painting some other part of the picture.

The wise watercolorist will take advantage of the rapid, fluid nature of his medium to capture his model's most lively—sometimcs fleeting—expression.

Many decisions and pitfalls that might delay the painting may be forestalled in the course of the drawing, which is dealt with in the next chapter.

P.F. and D.S.

CHAPTER VIII

THE DRAWING

WHILE A painting may not show so much as a single pencil stroke, it is, nevertheless, based on a definite drawing that may exist on paper or merely in the mind of the artist. In the more opaque mediums an elaborate design may be made, then covered up as the painting progresses. The transparent qualities of watercolor, however, prevent this. A minimum of lines is required; the fewer the better.

Because of this limitation, the drawing must be carefully thought out and visualized as a whole before the paper is touched. Each line must have a specific purpose in the construction of the composition. It should be definite and telling, showing that the painter is sure of his purpose (see Plate 11). A sketchy, searching line is seldom successful as a foundation for a portrait.

The drawing for a watercolor portrait should act principally as a guide on which to hang the painting. With the exception of a few lines that may be left to point up important planes or angles, it should be considered more or less of a scaffolding to be removed once its function is served. These lines should be drawn lightly with a soft pencil—3B to 6B—so that they may be removed later with an artgum without too much scrubbing. This is especially important in the intermediate values. Pencil marks may be erased from a light portion or covered with paint in the dark areas, but an erasure in a middle tone will usually lighten the paint also. It may be noted here that erasures preceding the painting should be kept to a minimum, for, though artgum is comparatively soft, too many or too vigorous rubbings may remove the sizing and damage the paper surface, causing the fiber to absorb paint too readily. An interesting departure from the pencil is the use of the fine-pointed brush and a painted line, which is illustrated in Phoebe Flory's "Listening" (Plate 28).

Thinking of the setup in terms of volume rather than flat pattern, the artist should indicate the placement of important areas, such as the head and shoulders, and, perhaps, an arm and hand, if they are to be included, and any dominant design in the background that may serve to complement the mass of the figure.

After the pose has been carefully considered, the artist may wish to exaggerate certain directions for the sake of balance. He may distort some particular line or lines to achieve emphasis through repetition or opposition.

Next the features are blocked in. Some think it helpful to sketch them in planes, while others find a mere suggestion of placement sufficient. This drawing "shorthand" often seems to encourage greater freedom in painting and prevents the possibility of the drawing being used as a crutch. When done in planes, the angles may be softened and rounded prior to painting, though this is not necessary.

There have been numerous sets of rules offered for the general placement and relative proportion of the various features. Some of these rules, dealing with a standard head, are occasionally helpful; but their fallacy lies in the fact that few subjects conform to the hypothetical norm. Consequently, the drawings of an artist who concentrates on a standard formula of measurements tend to pull toward that common denominator and to possess a "family resemblance." In order to bring out the individuality of subjects, we feel it is better to concentrate on the *differences* among people, rather than on their similarities.

Compared to other heads you have observed, is this one round, square, oval, or triangular? Does it rest on a neck that is short and thick, or long and slender? Is the front plane of the forehead narrow and high, or is it a broad expanse across the face? Is the brow shallow, or prominent, jutting out over deep eye sockets? Are the cheekbones high and sharp? Where is the eye line in relation to the sphere of the head? What is the distance between the eyes? Are the nostrils flaring or narrow? Is the mouth generous and full or tight and pinched? Is the hairline receding or low, and does it coincide with the angle between the forehead and the top plane of the head?

All these the artist must ask himself, then check and recheck, for one misplaced line can destroy a likeness. He should compare distances against distances, by eye alone, and, if need be, by checking them with the aid of measurements on a pencil held at arm's length.

When the structure of the head and body is satisfactorily drawn, further lines should be added to indicate the principal shadows. They should, by no means, outline a shaded area or separate light from shadow, but should serve merely as a guide to suggest their general direction and proportions.

Should the beginner find that he is having difficulty, or that his eraser is being overworked, he would do well to make several drawings of the head and portions of the head from different views before beginning to paint.

D.S.

CHAPTER IX

DIRECT PAINTING IN BLACK AND WHITE

To paint a watercolor directly means to achieve in one drying period the values and colors that you intend for the finished work.

This can be accomplished even with the complexities of a watercolor portrait if you do not attempt to complete the entire picture (or even the entire head) in one drying time. You may, instead, divide it into sections, each section small enough for you to finish without hurrying.

As in most painting, you need have no difficulty in obtaining exactly the right value in one shot if you first learn to paint in black and white. Alberti, in the fifteenth century, wrote:

> I certainly agree that abundance and variety of colors contribute greatly to the charm and beauty of the picture. But I would have artists be convinced that the supreme skill and art in painting consists in knowing how to use black and white. And every effort and diligence is to be employed in learning the correct use of these two pigments.

Learning to work in black and white is not, however, just an exercise. Some of the most finished and powerful painting in history was done entirely in monochrome: witness the great Chinese art, or the Western Dürer, Blake, and Daumier. There are some, indeed, who be-

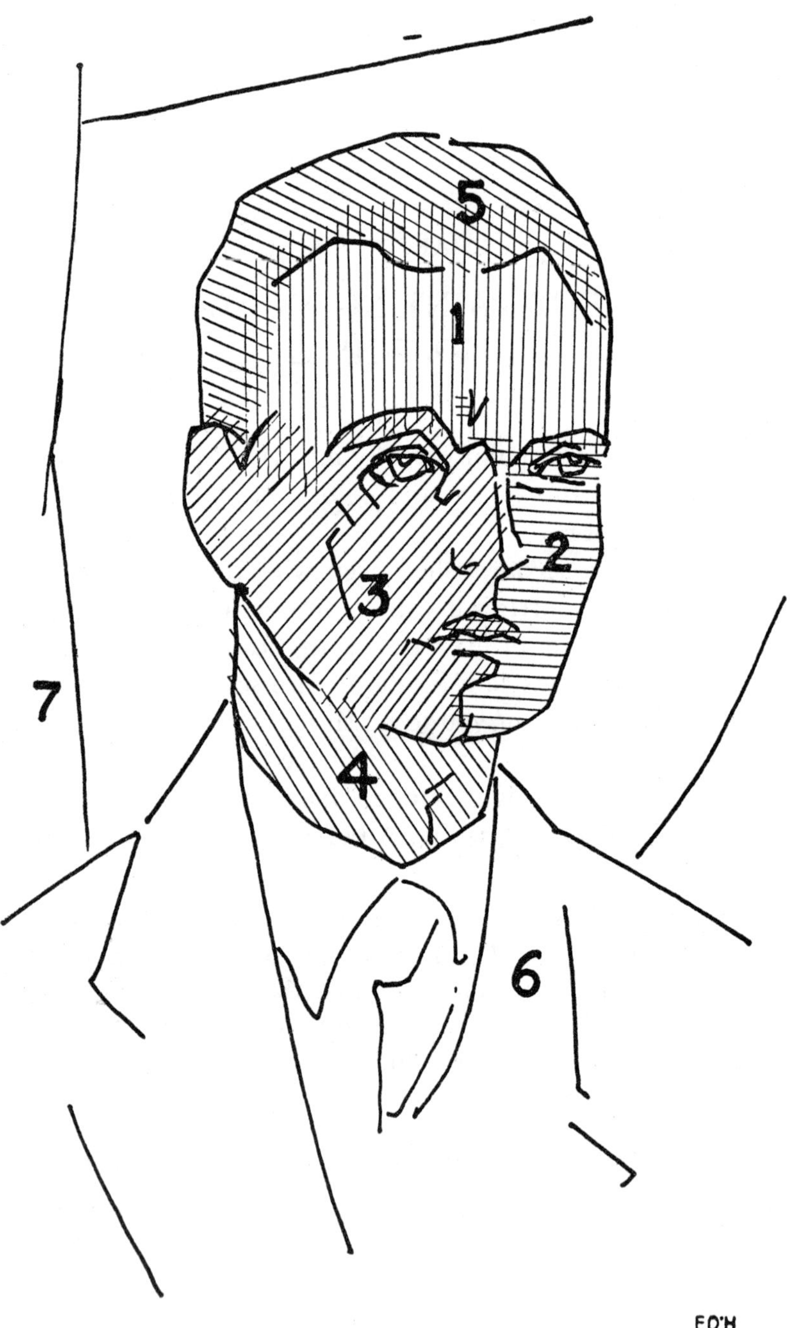

PLATE 12. Eliot O'Hara. Plan of Painting Sequence for "Returned Veteran"

In direct painting, sections are completed in one drying period.

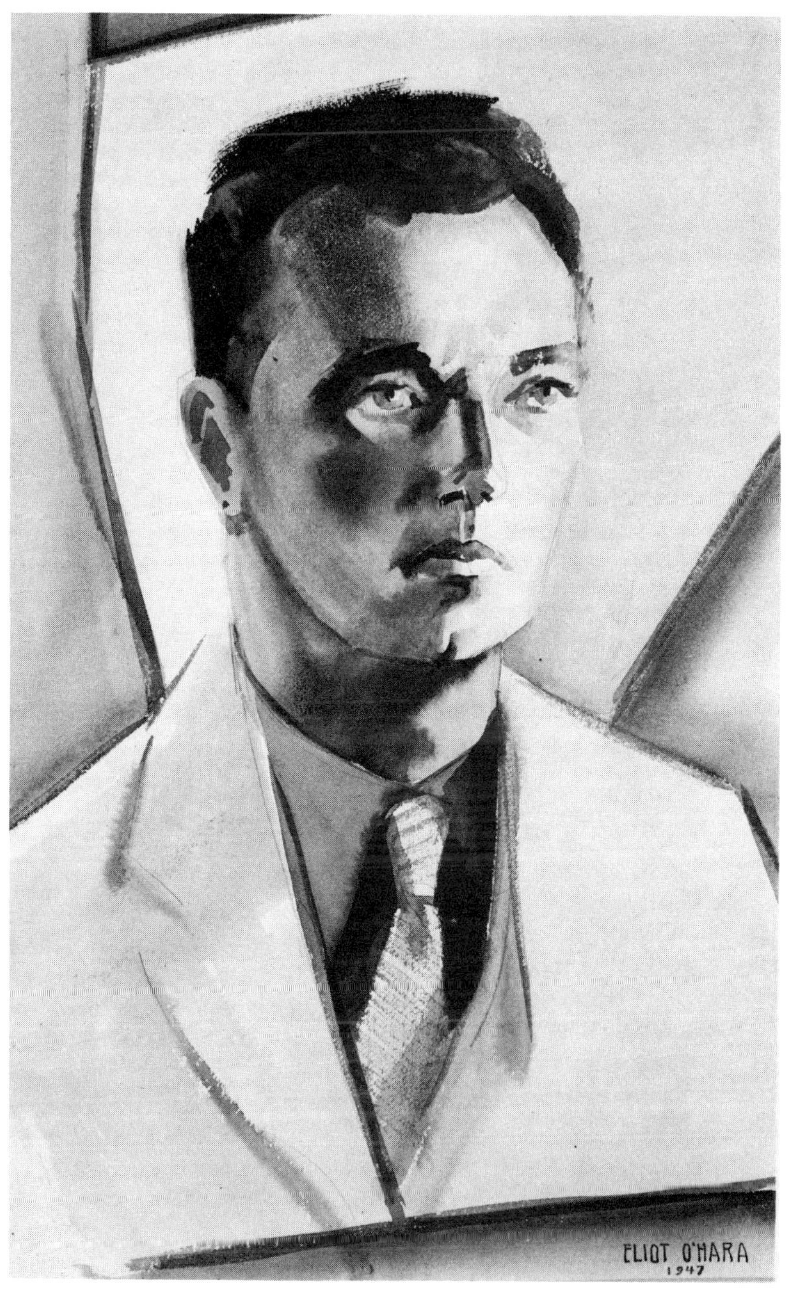

PLATE 13. Eliot O'Hara: "Returned Veteran." One-hour class demonstration for direct painting.

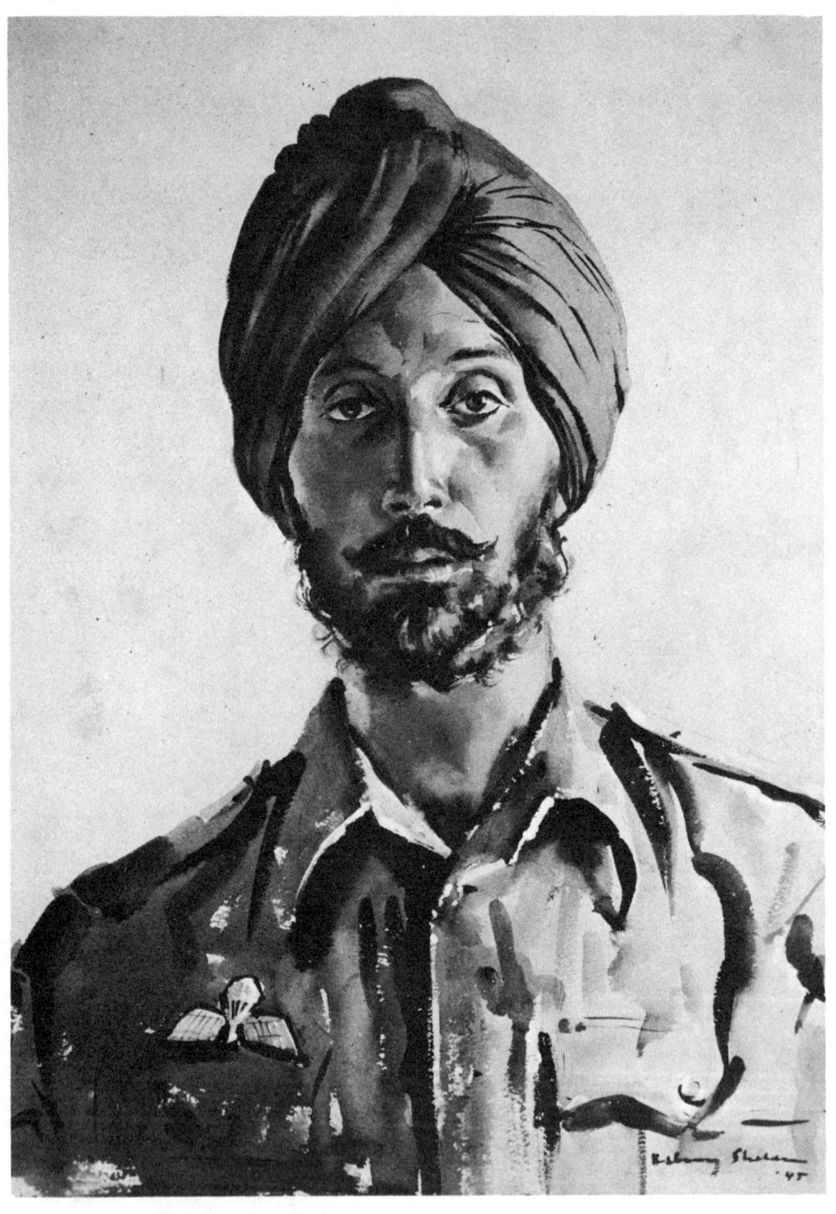

PLATE 14. H. Harry Sheldon: "A Sikh Paratrooper." A distinguished contemporary example of England's traditional medium. *Courtesy, the Earl Mountbatten of Burma.*

lieve that painting in tones is the purest form of art, and that color is superfluous, just as they feel that chamber music is the purest form of music and a full symphony is overelaboration. Whether or not you agree, it is certainly practical to master painting in black and white as it will always be useful in book and fashion illustration, commercial and advertising art, cartoons and caricatures. You can make your light and dark as well as your texture design so telling that no color is needed.

In order to concentrate on painting technique in this first portrait, simplify as much as possible all other problems—of drawing, lighting, and design. Later you need not, and should not, hold yourself to these restrictions.

Include just the head and shoulders. As it is more difficult to show the volume of a head if you see it in profile or full front, select the view somewhere between, which we call the three-quarter view.

Since two or more lights from different directions confuse the planes, use a single source of light, a window or spot light. If it illuminates the far side of the model's face, as it did in the case of "Returned Veteran" by Eliot O'Hara (Plate 13), you will see, on the near side, both shadow and reflected light, which will help you to model the form.

Avoid the complications of perspective that you will have if you are looking down or up at your subject. Make it easy for yourself this time by having his head straight and on a level with yours.

On a sheet of rough paper at least fifteen by eighteen inches, draw him close to life size, so that you will not be cramped by modeling diminutive planes on an undersized drawing.

To adhere very long to these simplified conditions will

make a very dull series of portraits. They are advocated now merely to allow you to concentrate, in this first full portrait, on painting technique.

Now that you have cleared the decks of everything else that might distract you, you are ready to plan the painting.

First, lightly with your pencil, divide your drawing into sections. Each section should be no larger than you can complete comfortably in one drying time. As the edges of the divisions may show a little, look for natural boundaries. You might do the face in three parts. Eyebrows, for example, may be a natural dividing line between the forehead and lower face. The nose is a natural division between the far and near cheeks.

Since there is no natural boundary between the mouth and cheeks, you may arbitrarily set your division at the edge of a shadow: the point at which the illuminated plane of the mouth and chin turns into the shaded side. This line will curve to follow the form of the lips and chin, as it does in the diagram, Plate 12, of the painting sequence for "Returned Veteran."

You have now divided the face into three parts: (1) forehead, (2) far side of the face, and (3) near side of the face. The other sections are easy: (4) neck, (5) hair, (6) shoulders, and (7) background. No one area is larger than you can complete comfortably in one drying period.

In order to swing easily into painting, it is wise, at this point, to take a separate sheet and practice cylinders and domes, modeling with washes from light to dark, and into reflected light. When you allow the model to take a rest, in order to duplicate the lighting on him, set up in his place some cylindrical and dome-shaped forms. Practice on these until you are ready to resume the portrait.

There is no need to hurry. Remember that you may

continue modifying a wash as long as you keep the paper wet. You need not do it in one stroke. If you dampen the paper first you can add paint or take it away, thus achieving the right value until you allow it to dry.

To arrive at the right value you must keep two things in mind: first, that the wet paint appears darker than it will when it is dry; second, that a section surrounded by clean paper looks darker (in contrast to the white) than it will later in the finished picture. This means that you must visualize the whole picture, and the first area that you paint must relate to the as-yet-unpainted surroundings. For this reason, the first section is usually the most difficult, and furthermore it sets the scale of values for the entire picture. Start, therefore, with the easiest part of the face, which is the forehead. It is a simple rounded form turning from light into shadow and then into reflected light.

Reserving white paper for the highlight, scumble around it with the lightest wash, then blend it smoothly into the shadow. Since pigment will dry much lighter, exaggerate the shadow and be sure that you make the reflected light several degrees darker than the highlight.

If your subject's hair is darker than his skin, slightly emphasize the forehead shadows lest, later, in contrast to the hair, they appear too light.

Where the forehead ends decisively, as on the bone at the far side, or where it may be covered, as by eyebrows, you may leave a hard line, but elsewhere taper off the wash. Carry the wash of the forehead far up under the hairline and back at the sides, as the scalp will show through the darker hair. If you leave a sharp edge along the entire hairline it will look like a wig.

If his flesh is darker than his hair, as it may well be if he is very blond or white haired, fade the flesh tone off gradually at the hairline and not beyond it. The hairline will be soft where the flesh shows through and sharper where a lock of hair falls over the forehead.

Then carry the wash at the temples down past the eyebrows, and let it fade off to nothing. You probably need some warning that at this point the portrait will look very peculiar, but don't be dismayed. The actual face of the model would be equally appalling if parts were missing.

You can paint a watercolor in sections and not have it look all chopped up if you have mastered the problems in splicing explained in Chapter VI on "Modeling with Paint." Just as the cabinetmaker tapers two boards to a wedge and overlaps them so that the combined wedges are no thicker than the boards, you can taper the edge of one wash off to nothing and let it dry completely, before overlapping the next wash, light at first (where you are double painting) and gradually darker as it covers virgin paper.

Remember, however, that in a watercolor you cannot work over an area of dry paint very long before you begin to loosen the pigment underneath, so do not dampen the seams until you are ready to join them. If you are doing, for example, the near side of the face, which in this case is in shadow (section 3 in the diagram, Plate 12), wet the paper only up to, and not overlapping, the forehead wash at the temples (section 1). When you are finished with section 3, clean your brush and drag a little of the shadow up and overlap the forehead tone. With skill the two portions can be spliced without showing the seam.

But perhaps your forehead area is not yet dry. While

you are waiting for it, skip the near side of the face and do the far side (section 2).

When you paint the far side of the face take into consideration the value of the hair or background behind it. Since too sharp a contrast at the edge will make the far side appear to come forward rather than turn back, a slightly darker tone as it curves will help to ease the transition and to turn the plane.

Making sure that the eye shadow is dark enough, carry the face washes over the entire area of the eye, as it is the deepest indentation in the face, and even though the eyeball and lips protrude, they usually have some shadow cast by the surrounding bony structure. You may ignore the highlight in the eye; it can be added later if at all. Model the eyeball and lids in masses rather than lines, and omit all but the most significant details. While the eye area is still damp, spot in the iris and the lashes of the upper lid. You can often omit the lower lashes entirely, relying on planes rather than a line for modeling the lower lid. Understate the shadows at the nasal fold and at the corners of the mouth for they add age and suggest an unpleasant disposition.

Since by now the forehead is completely dry, you can proceed to the near side of the face. Refer to the forehead for your scale of values in the shadow and reflected light; remembering to allow for the tones fading as they dry.

When you paint the mouth and chin section ignore the local color of the lips. Paint over the entire mouth area, just as you did over the entire eye socket, with skin tone, modeling the form first. Then add the darker lip values while the underlying area is still damp, so that they will blend softly and avoid the "pasted on" look that cheapens a portrait.

Before finishing the near side of the face and while the

wash is still wet, drag a little of the pigment up to overlap the forehead.

Simplify the cylinder form of the neck (section 4). A too detailed realism of cords and cartilage adds age and detracts from the face.

When you come to the hair, consider it in planes, top, front, and sides, and the underneath planes, which receive the light differently. Since the hair is a mass, even if not solid, the lighting follows form and not direction of the growth of hair, just as in painting fields of grass the planes may be horizontal although the texture is vertical. Wet blend the light and dark form first, and add texture second.

Where the hair grows down over the skin of forehead and temples, soften the edge by dampening it first with clear water and allowing the hair tone to flow into the dampened area. Only a slight amount of water is necessary to soften the line. Too much will form a puddle and the paint will flow all the way to the edge forming another hard line. Or you may use the alternate method of softening the sharp hairline by wiping it out before it is dry.

The shoulders (section 6), also, should be simplified in planes. If they are turned, make the far one go back by being lighter or darker than the near one. The relationship of the shoulders and the background wash may also be varied from one side to the other.

After you have finished the background (section 7), take a rest, so that you may study the picture with a fresh eye. Perhaps it is finished. It is possible to include all the details necessary when you are treating each area. The eyebrows can be wet blended onto the forehead, the opening of the nostrils when you paint the nose.

If after you rest, however, you still feel the need for

more details, select them carefully and include only the most significant. Adding all the details you can think of may complete the realism of the picture, but too many will kill its freshness and the quality of suggestion so important in a portrait. Do not salt and pepper the picture, after it is dry, with a lot of sharp accents.

The next time you paint a direct watercolor portrait you may wish to vary the order of the sections, starting, perhaps, with the broadest areas of background and clothes and to work inward to the detailed portions of the head. Or you may wish to spot in the darks first, to have a value target at which to aim.

When you have become familiar with the procedure, you may branch out to try different poses, lighting, backgrounds, and perspective. Finally, you may apply the same procedure to portraits in full color, as will be described in Chapter XI.

Before, however, embarking on color, it is well to explore the possibilities of texture interest, as H. Harry Sheldon may have done before painting his "Sikh Paratrooper" (Plate 14). A series of portraits executed in smooth washes will be stamped with as much monotony as portraits with uniform lighting or standard compositions. After studying the next chapter, therefore, on "Surface Textures," you will be able to add yet another enrichment to your black and white portraits, which you may later carry over into color.

P.F.

CHAPTER X

SURFACE TEXTURES

WHILE ONE may paint a picture of a person in flat uneven tones, and it may be an interesting pattern and a good likeness, certain other elements are needed to make it a vibrant portrait. Among these is surface texture. It helps to turn the form, and furnishes the tactile quality that gives vitality to the painting.

Painters often overstep the bounds of one medium and combine several for the purpose of increasing the range of textures. Some even go so far as to paste on the canvas such extraneous materials as rope, wire, and cloth, to achieve the desired effect. One need not, however, go to such extremes to attain interest successfully within a single medium.

Watercolor affords an opportunity for achieving an almost unlimited variety of textures. In addition to numerous modifications of the simple brush stroke, there are, at the artist's disposal, qualities resulting from the manipulation of such tools as the knife, the bristle brush, the rag, and the finger.

A diversity of texture adds interest to a painting by relieving monotony and by qualifying the nature of the different surfaces. The "feel" of the skin may be made to differ from the "feel" of the hair. A tweed cloth may exhibit its distinctive roughness in comparison to the gleaming smoothness of satin. This variety serves to con-

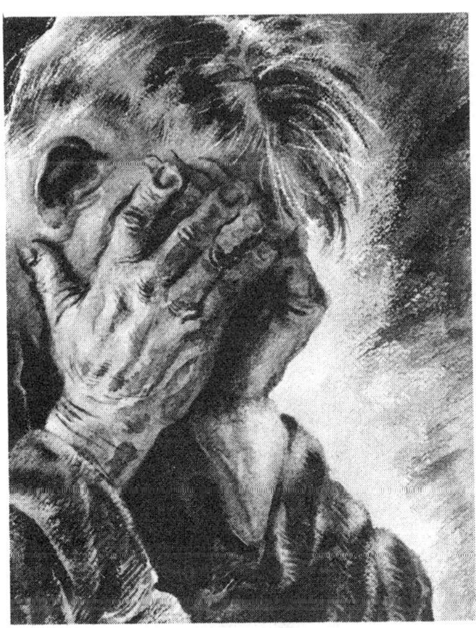

PLATE 15. Greta Matson: "Grief"—detail. Knifing, rough-brushed overpainting, and scraping. (See Plate 43.)

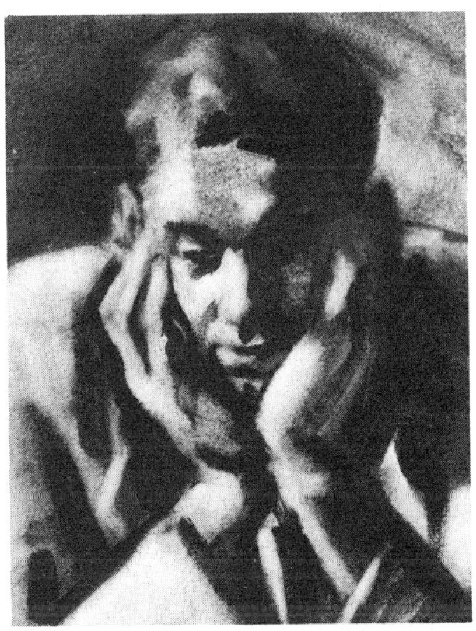

PLATE 16. J. C. McPherson: "Watercolor Portrait." Color flooded into and wiped out of soaked paper.

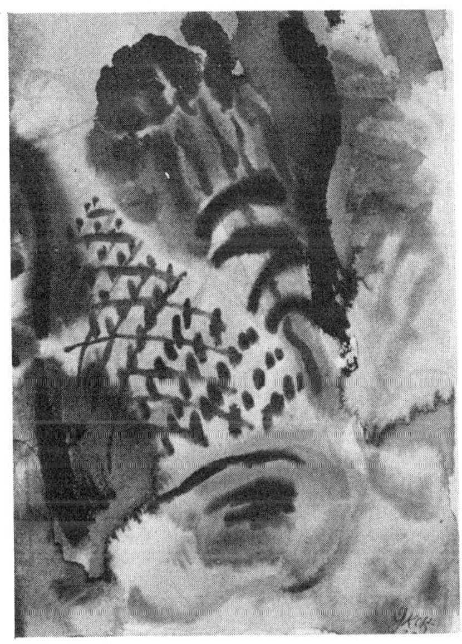

PLATE 17. George Grosz: "Rotisserie"—detail. Wet-blended textures and "oozles." *Courtesy, Mrs. Solomon Diamond. Photograph courtesy Associated American Artists Galleries.* (See Plate 32.)

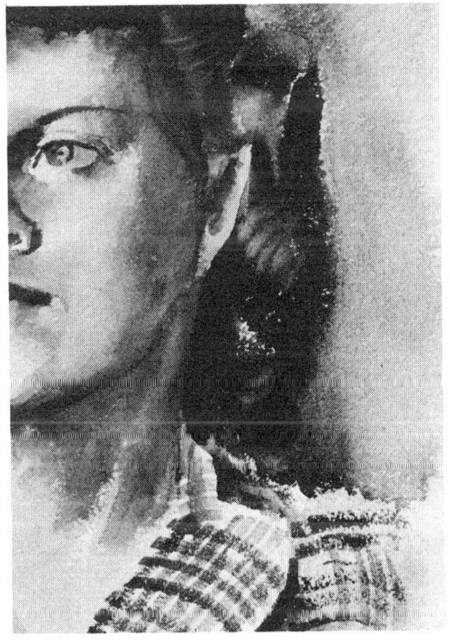

PLATE 18. Phoebe Flory: "Girl in Plaid"—detail. Rough brushing, whisking, and divided-hair strokes. (See Plate 34)

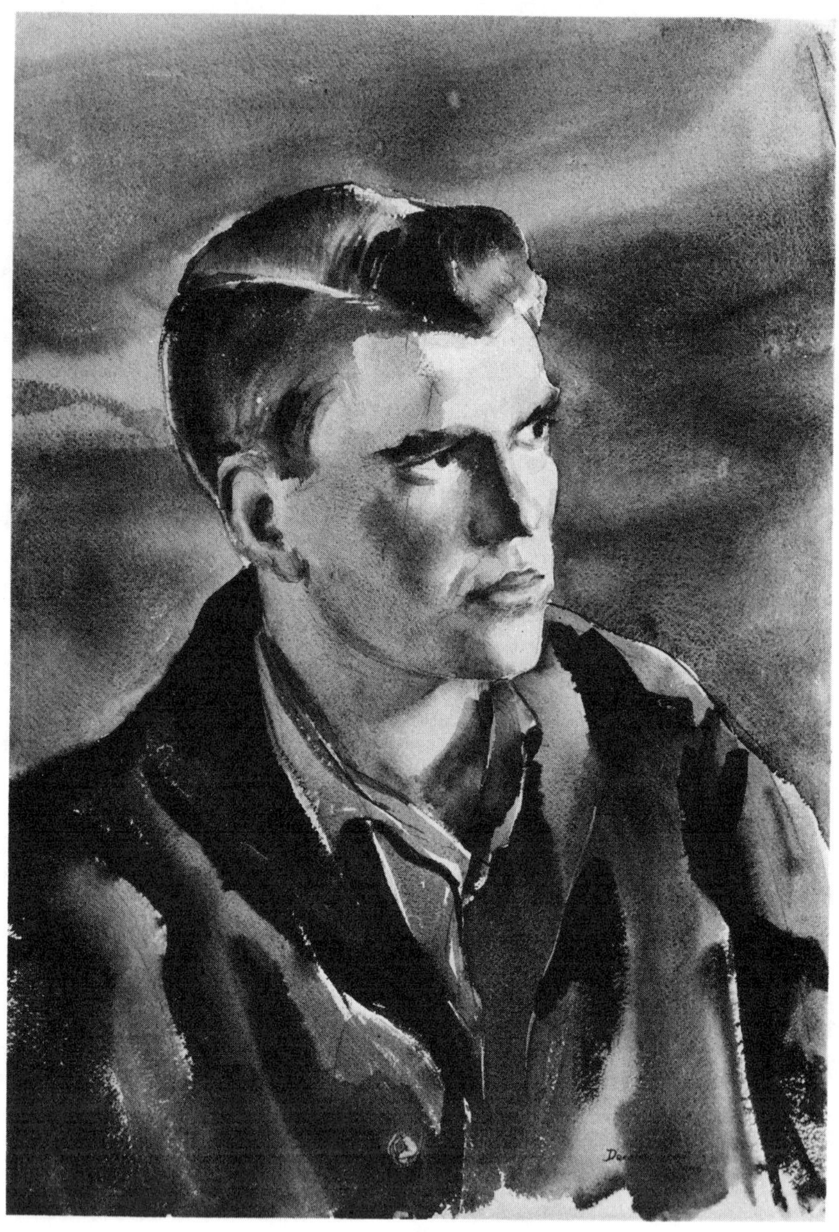

PLATE 19. Dorothy Short: "Armed Guard." A direct laying-on of washes, with darks reinforced while the areas were still wet.

tribute a live quality to a work that might otherwise be dull and uninteresting.

Like everything else, however, texture can be overdone. Discretion should be exercised to avoid an overly ornate surface treatment, or the painting will have the appearance of a brush drill. The heavily worked areas should be carefully distributed as one would distribute values in a composition, to achieve balance. Just as a room decorated with a few prints or stripes combined with some plain materials is to be preferred to one decorated completely in pattern, so the portrait in which texture is used with restraint is preferable to one that is cluttered with it.

It is wise, when planning a painting, to arrange a repeat of some design. This tends to strengthen the balance of the composition, and aids in establishing the "path of the eye." Greta Matson's "Grief" (Plates 15 and 43) adequately illustrates this quality, which serves to enhance the mood of the painting.

Texture in dress may be used to advantage to set off the simple wash of the skin, or a rough-surfaced area of the hair, to contrast with a wet-blended background. The background, often the most abstract portion of the portrait, offers an extraordinary opportunity for the use of surface texture. When it is treated last, it may serve to contrast, to soften, to key, or to pull together the already painted head and dress.

Sometimes grain is used simply to vary an abstract area and to relieve its plainness. By blotting with a squeezed-out brush or sponge, the artist may contribute an interesting pattern to a background or portion of the clothing. He can achieve surface character by unlimited means. There are no set rules, and no holds are barred.

The knife will prove a useful tool, but it must be used

correctly for the desired results. It should be held at an acute angle to the surface of the paper, then drawn along, like a butter spreader, in the direction of the slant, to remove paint and clear a path of clean paper. If the blade is held at right angles to the paper, like a razor, it will scar and roughen the surface without scraping it clean of paint.

Different effects may be achieved by knifing on very wet, moderately damp, and completely dry surfaces. A knife scraped over a wet surface will merely take off the sizing and allow the tinted water to soak in and darken the strip. When the paper has reached the proper stage of dryness, a knife stroke will remove paint from a half-dry surface and leave the area white with clean, sharp edges. If the paper is too damp, the edges will be fuzzy and uneven. Used on a dry surface, the blade removes a small portion of the particles and lightens the area (see Plate 15). Pigment colors are more easily removed than staining colors. In fact, if a surface is painted first with a staining color, you can knife down to it as if to white paper, removing the pigments but not the stain.

The use of the knife is more appropriate in certain portions of the portrait than others. It is not always wise to use it where the substance is soft and pliable, as in hair, unless the latter is short and crisp.

Knifing should never be used to scrape large areas where a smooth effect is desired, but should be reserved for accents and lines. A large area, however, may be enhanced and lightened through the use of tiny crosshatched strokes. For the highlight in the eyes, the blade should be pressed hard in order to remove the entire top layer of paper and leave the surface pure white. A razor may also flick out highlights. Moist paint may also be scraped away by softer instruments, which do not scar the surface, such as a rubber sink scraper or an orangewood sculptor's tool (carved to the proper shape).

One may achieve other effects by sprinkling into a half-dry wash drops of water from the fingers or a brush. These spread and bloom into a fluid pattern, forming what we call "oozles." The long flexible rigger is excellent for uneven or wriggly lines, effective in the painting of hair or cloth as in Phoebe Flory's "Girl in Plaid" (Plates 18 and 34), and as in "Rotisserie" by George Grosz (Plates 17 and 32). The design is drawn into the drying wash with the brush containing clear or colored water. Moisture introduced into a still damp area has the effect of spreading the not-yet-dry particles of paint away from the center of the newly wet portion and depositing them on top of the surrounding rim of pigment. Just the right amount of water is required. Too much would swamp the area and defeat the purpose.

The impression of cloth with a heavy nap may be achieved by reinforcing an already dry wash with rough brushing or a network of crosshatching (Plates 18 and 34). Squeeze the brush almost dry, so that the hairs are slightly separated; then supply it with paint and draw it across the surface of rough-textured paper, or, holding the brush vertically, whisk it on smooth paper. Depending on the amount of paint and the amount of water, the result on rough paper will be either a series of whiskings or a rough, speckled pattern.

"Rough brushing" is accomplished by drawing a moderately dry brush across rough paper. The brush is held either parallel to the paper or at a sharp angle to it. The rough brushing will be blurred if the base surface is at all moist.

A double-loaded brush, containing one color on one side and another on the other, may be useful, possibly for describing certain patterns in cloth. It may also serve to model, in one stroke, any small rounded form.

The practice of wiping out wet paint with a dry brush is often a successful means for achieving texture, as in J. C. McPherson's "Watercolor Portrait" (Plate 16). This may be done evenly with a brush—as if applying paint—or can be blotted and smeared by pressing the hairs into the paper and causing an irregular design. On rough paper, make your wipe-outs just after the sheen has disappeared but before the paper is dry. On smooth paper, make your wipe-outs before the sheen is gone. You may, however, remove paint from smooth paper that has entirely dried by redamping the area.

In order to improve your versatility and to enlarge your technical vocabulary, you would do well to devote yourself occasionally to simple exercises on surface texture. By relying on your previously acquired facility with tools, you may let your imagination run riot. As a preliminary exercise, the making of samples is most helpful. Cut into strips, approximately three by eight inches, some watercolor paper with a definite grain, and some very smooth paper. (Smooth paper affords radically different effects—among them cleaner, sharper wipe-outs, knifings, and oozles.) After these tryouts, you may put your results to use on a painting. Select a portrait that is dull from sameness and copy it. Your object is to enliven it simply through the use of varied and interesting surface treatment. Texture quickies preliminary to the final painting will also prove profitable.

Now, having become familiar with this addition to your watercolor vocabulary, turn to the next chapter, "Direct Painting in Color," and make use of your added skill.

D.S.

CHAPTER XI

DIRECT PAINTING IN COLOR

THE DIRECT approach in watercolor may be described as first cousin to the "quickie" (Chapter XIV), for the two treatments possess, to an unusual degree, the common qualities of spontaneity and clarity. They also share certain difficulties and problems. Chief among these is the necessity for "getting it right the first time." Like the quickie, the direct approach demands the exceptional in dexterity and requires that the painter have at his finger tips a knowledge of all the different treatments, and the ability to put them to instant use. Because there may be no overpainting, his first decision must be correct. Consequently, he should strive to bring this difficult technique within his control and to apply the resulting sureness of handling and immediate evaluation of color to other painting approaches. Thus, it becomes not only an end in itself, but also an exercise for training purposes.

As you will remember in Chapter IX, "Direct Painting in Black and White," this method, unlike some of the more specialized ones, combines the qualities of all watercolor, and permits a maximum of effect through the interplay of contrasting textures and treatments. Differing from the quickie, the direct approach has the advantage of several drying periods, making possible a more deliberate pace.

Having attained sufficient facility in black and white,

you may wish to attempt a direct painting in full color.

Before beginning the actual painting, however, it is advisable to assemble in your mind the elements required in building this picture.

Review: (1) The structure of body and head, noting peculiarities of the figure before you.

(2) Your lesson on "Modeling with Paint," for facility in achieving smooth, evenly graded washes, and accustoming yourself to the handling of turning surfaces and the invisible "splice."

(3) Your black and white direct paintings, planning changes you may wish to make and ways to avoid repetition of unfortunate accidents.

This is the time to formulate in your mind a definite color scheme for a composition. First determine the general complexion type; then plan your method of approach in order to express this type convincingly. Regardless of the kind of skin, color changes, due to physical structure, blood supply, etc., take place in every face. In general, in light-skinned people the forehead appears somewhat orange, the cheek portion, reddish, and the neck and the area surrounding the mouth, yellowish, even greenish, in tone. A cooler tint is often found in the eyelids and the hollow of the eye, especially in people with thin, transparent skin. The nose and ears are constructed of cartilage, through which light may be seen, which gives these features a definite, and often vivid, red coloring. In subjects with pale, fair skin, the blues and violets are likely to predominate, and the areas in direct light may be pure white. The eyelids and nostrils will appear more transparent, and the whole effect will be one of delicacy. There is, of course, a kind of skin that is light, but thick and pasty, and lacks this delicate transparent quality. In subjects with olive complexions, yellow tends to influence all the facial color changes, making the portion in direct light warm and all blues and violets lean toward green or, in some cases, even brown. Ruddy complexions are affected similarly by red, and the greens and yellows are subordinated. It must be remembered that these color traits are rarely found in intense saturated tones. Black should be avoided in hair as it is a dead pigment. A more lively substitute is a combination of burnt umber, burnt sienna, dioxazime purple, phthalocyanine blue or green and indigo.

The same wide variety of color exists among people of the darker races. They are not simply "black," and black pigment is best not used, since, as just mentioned, it has a deadening effect. You will find some individuals who tend toward the warmer tones—oranges or brown, depending on the value of the complexion, and others, often those who are darker-skinned, who lean toward violet. In any case, the highlights are usually cool by comparison. The ears are pinker than the face, just as they are in lighter-skinned people, and the lips are usually pink and frequently lighter than the surrounding area. Often there is a bright red line between the lips where the surface is moist. The lips are generally fuller than in most white-skinned people, so the correct placement of the highlight is especially important, to describe the distinctive contour. Since the hair is usually not smooth, it will probably have a diffused highlight and it must be modeled carefully in order to indicate the shape of the head.

Having completed your drawing and color decisions, you are ready to undertake the actual painting. First, however, there are several facts and suggestions worthy of mention.

1. Because watercolor lightens as it dries, and because, in this method, darks may not be reinforced after they are dry, paint your values darker than you see them and darker than you wish them to appear later.

2. Avoid a preponderance of sharp edges to prevent a

"cut-out" look; strive for subtle transitions and "lost and found" edges, by means of varying the line. In general, the outline of the face is sharp where bone is near the surface, soft where fatty tissues pad the frame.

3. Details in shadow are less sharply defined than those in light.

4. Some people prefer to understate the value of shadows (unless a particularly dramatic effect is desired), since lighter washes tend to be more transparent than dark ones, and are more easily handled. If a proper value relationship is established, moderately toned shadows will give the impression of being darker than they actually are.

When the drawing is completed, the composition should be divided into sections, as described in Chapter IX. These divisions, you will recall, are made to permit individual treatment of each area. Never, if it can be avoided, should there be a separation within a smooth area. If the painter so desires, he may devote an entire drying period to each section. The more sections he can handle in one period, however, the better.

He is now confronted with the task of uniting adjacent areas. If they are still wet, he may simply blend them. After the first portion has begun to dry, however, the artist must wait until it is completely dry, then either overlap a wash or fuse the two with a brush held vertically and squeezed dry enough to cause a whisking stroke of fine, hairlike lines. In any case, no separating spaces are desirable.

In order to discuss the approach, let us now assume the following conditions. These are identical with those existing in the illustration, "Armed Guard" (Plate 19), a portrait of a young man with strong, well-defined features.

The model is posed so as to be at a three-quarter-degree

angle from the artist, and faces the artist's right. The source of light existing at the model's left causes a shadow on the model's right (near) side. A reflecting surface casts a secondary light, so the shadow remains darkest down the nearest edge of the front plane of the face. The highlight falls on the "corner" of the forehead as it turns around the skull, down the center of the nose, on the upper lip, on the rounded upper side of the chin, and on a point above the near cheekbone.

Because the board is tilted, causing water to flow toward the painter, and because of the structural simplicity of the forehead, the painting of that portion is usually undertaken first.

The highlight is left unpainted and the wash either blended (by surrounding the highlight with clean water, then introducing color), or rough brushed around it. The transition must be gradual, not sharp, or the effect of the skin will be lost. The wash then is carried across the area and onto the side plane, which later in the same drying period receives a superimposed shadow. Because the skull is a sphere, it curves at the top and bottom as well as at the sides. Consequently, there must be a tone to describe the contour. From the forehead, the skin tones should be carried into and beyond the hairline, so as to prevent any white paper from showing through the sparsely covered hair area, which is later reinforced by rough brushing or whisking to indicate hair. If the hair is lighter in value than the skin, it may be advisable to treat it first. A slightly darker and warmer tone just below the hairline suggests shadow cast by hair. Since shadows cast on smooth skin may have sharp edges, they may be superimposed over the original wash.

The next division may include the entire shaded side

of the face from browline to jawline, and contains usually the deepest and (indoors) warmest shadows (in the hollow between the bridge of the nose and the corner of the eye). The wash must cover the eye and the portion of the mouth in shadow, for even extremely light features in shadow will be darker; and the white of the eye contains a hint of the skin tone (or, in some instances, a bluish cast). The iris of the eye, the lips, and the eyebrows may be painted while the skin portion is wet, or may be superimposed later, if they are carefully blended with the initial wash, and the edges lost and found. Since the section must be completed within a single period, the darkest shadows should be reinforced while the surface is still wet. Or the darkest part of the shadow may be introduced first and the reflected light blended later as the brush passes across the area.

The neck comprises the third division. As in the face, the darkest part of the shadow exists just where it turns into the light. Should there be too subtle a difference between the neck and face to permit a separate treatment, at some point along the jawline the two areas must be blended as one, and a slight tone added, or a portion wiped out, to indicate reflected light. The neck itself should be simply modeled, so as not to detract from the forms of the face. While it is often yellowish in color, it is affected too, of course, by nearby reflecting surfaces. Its muscular structure should, in most cases, be merely suggested.

A pale tone—in daylight a cool flesh color—covers the illuminated side of the face and darkens as it turns the edges of the jaw and cheek. Darker still appear the isolated shadows in the eye socket, around the nostril, and, possibly, in the corner of the mouth. Should the light be

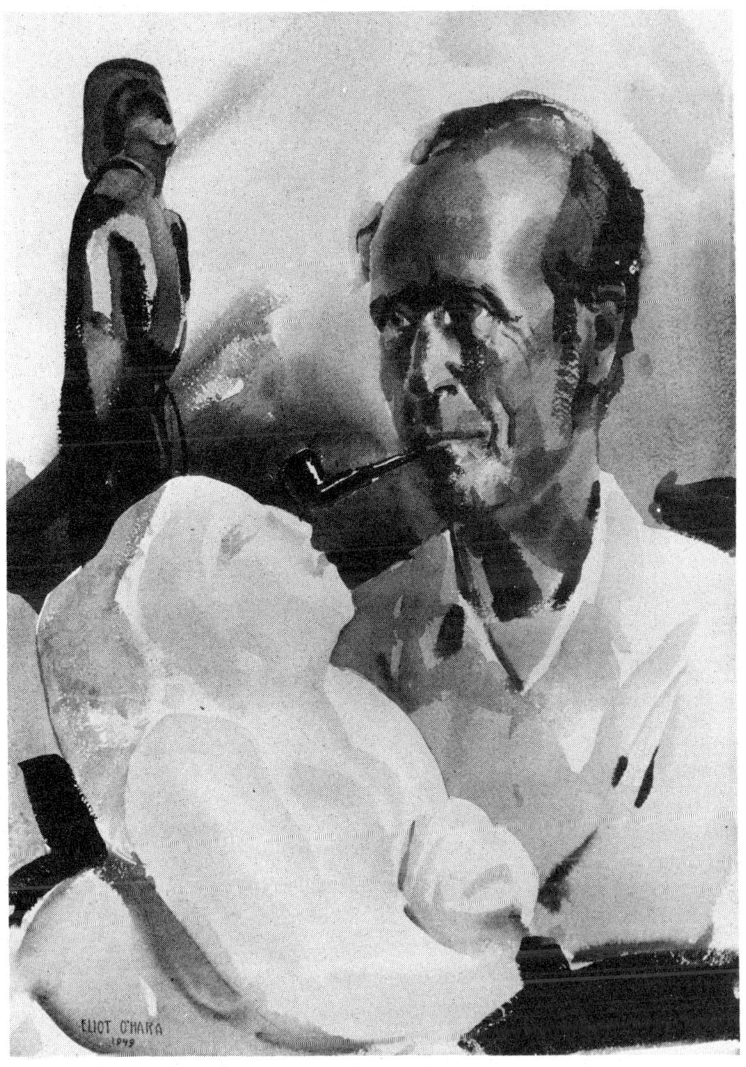

PLATE 20. Eliot O'Hara: "José de Creeft." Values and hues in ebony, marble, and flesh. (Reproduced in color on the front cover.)

strong enough to cause additional highlights on the nose, cheek, and chin, they should be treated like those on the forehead.

The artist should note the color differences among various portions of the figure and head, but, in painting them, should be careful not to overexaggerate. They must always be sufficiently related to indicate that they consist of the same substance. In his portrait of José de Creeft (Plate 20), Eliot O'Hara stressed variety in substances, where he juxtaposed the sculptor's work with the man himself.

The features should be painted in as broad a style as the large areas, and lines avoided. This is accomplished mainly through the use of the larger brushes. The shadows describing the curve of the folded eyelid, for example, may be painted in one stroke, and another stroke used to portray the fringe of lashes. While the iris of the eye may be painted over, and the highlight wiped out or added later with Chinese white, some artists prefer painting around the highlight, leaving it pure white paper. The shadow or crease extending from the nostril to the corner of the mouth should be understated to prevent the impression of a sneer, and the one at the corner of the mouth understated to avoid the effect of age. Only the line dividing the lips need be emphasized. In men, where the outlines of the lips are often indistinct, this is especially true.

The hair may be alternately blended or rough brushed and cut sharp against the washes of the skin to give a "growing" look. The outline of the hair, too, against the background, should be varied, to give the feeling of a head in space. Otherwise it may seem to be a flat object pasted against a flat surface. Shadows in blond hair are often green and in brunettes tend toward warm darks.

Highlights, on the other hand, are usually cool, even blue, in color.

The clothing may be treated as one division, or, if shadows and the design of the clothing permit, broken up into more than one and treated separately. The same is true of the background. Particularly if rough brushing is used, the divisions in the large area may be camouflaged and concealed. Grigory Gluckmann likes to blend figure into background with lost and found edges, as with his "Nude" (Plate 22).

There is sometimes an unconscious tendency on the part of the painter to consider the head the only really important part of a portrait. Actually, the clothing and background are of equal importance, not merely for themselves, but because they exert a tremendous influence on the already painted head. Should the artist find himself too tired or uninspired to concentrate after completing the face, he should put the painting aside until he is again stimulated and interested.

The apparel should be treated simply so as not to detract from the face, and each fold should explain the form beneath it.

The color should contribute to the general effect intended by the artist, and should never just happen. Avoid the habit of repeating the same background and clothing combinations in all your portraits. They are as individual as the complexions of your subjects, and should serve to complement them. Colors used for these areas may contrast, but should remain somewhat related to the skin tones, eyes, or hair. If the clothing is sheer, the warmth of the skin will, of course, show through. In nontransparent fabrics, also, a certain amount of warmth due to reflected light will exist where the material turns toward the skin, as at the neck, and on the underside of a fold.

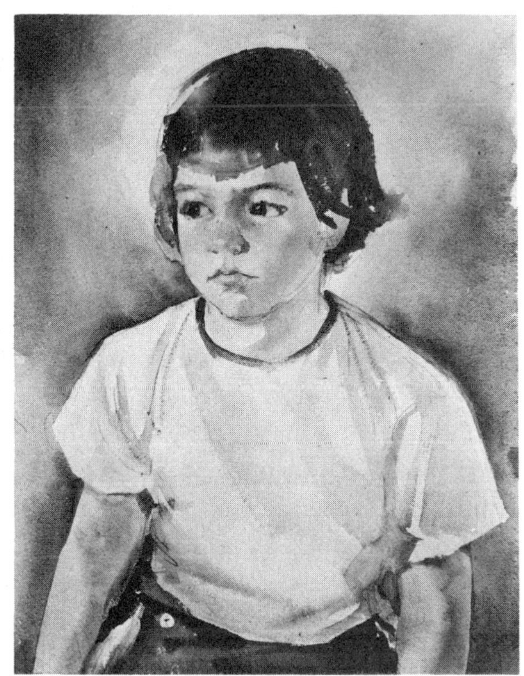

PLATE 21. Dorothy Short: "Growing Up." Watercolor lends itself to the fleeting quality of children.

PLATE 22. Grigory Gluckmann: "Nude." Edges lost and found through texture and values. *Courtesy, The Art Institute of Chicago.*

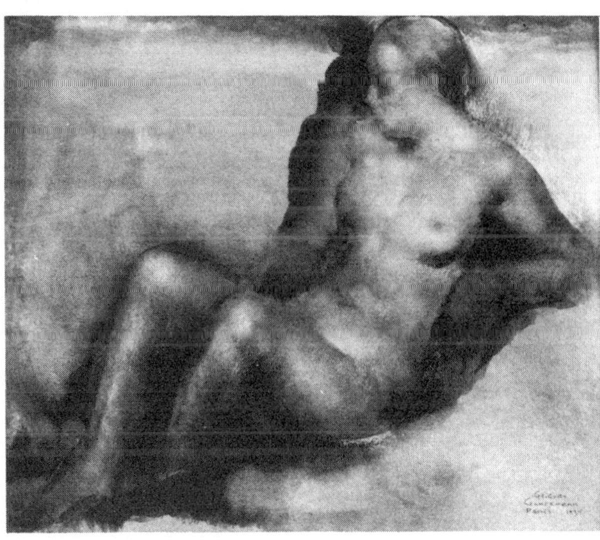

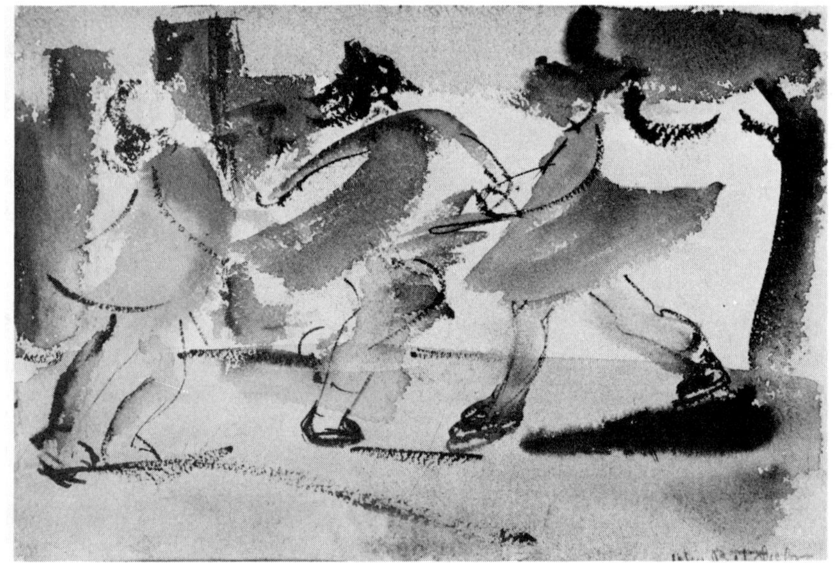

PLATE 23. Helen Batchelor: "Playtime." For motion—the quickie. *Courtesy, The Watercolor Gallery.*

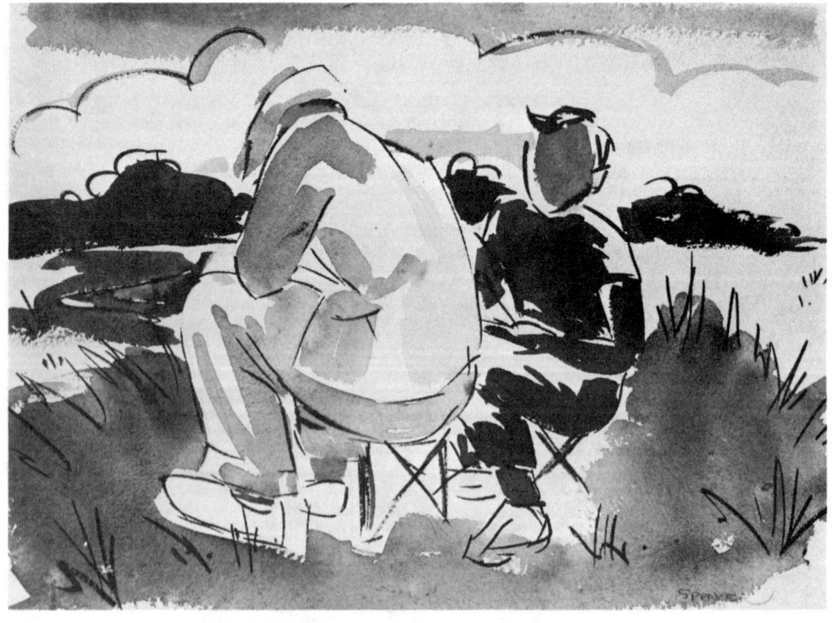

PLATE 24. Rebecca Spencer Files: "Sunday Painters." Freshness and boldness characterize the quickie. *Courtesy, The Watercolor Gallery.*

Design through the use of texture may serve to contrast and, therefore, heighten the smooth quality of the skin and hair. Personal taste will control the amount of elaboration. Because this method is one of the direct ones, there will be a minimum of underpainting. But, where a pattern of cloth is unusually pronounced, as, perhaps, in a distinct plaid of rough wool, there may be a ground wash reinforced by a series of rough brushed strokes, done with a dry brush that may be divided with the fingers or a pencil to give a striped effect. In her portrait, "Girl in Plaid," Phoebe Flory modeled the figure with a wash and superimposed the pattern of the cloth, part while the wash was still wet, and part when completely dry. The whisking stroke may serve to indicate threads or weave, and wet blending to describe the soft, rippling quality of velvet or satin.

Don't become so involved in cloth texture, however, that you sacrifice the fresh effect of the whole. Again the keynote is simplicity. This was my chief aim in painting the five-year-old, "Growing Up" (Plate 21).

In conclusion, let us bear in mind that the essentials for success in this method are: (1) freshness, achieved through smooth washes and determinate color; (2) variety, through texture; (3) contrast, through strong, well-balanced pattern; and (4) boldness, which is often responsible for the life and individuality of the portrait.

D.S.

CHAPTER XII

FIGURE QUICKIES

A FIGURE quickie, to the watercolorist, is a sketch of a figure painted in a limited period, without the use of pencil. More than any other treatment, the quickie is characterized by a casual, impromptu quality and an unwonted boldness.

Its purposes are to accustom one to speed, to train the eye, and to loosen the style. Speed, accuracy of perception, and facility of the hand are three factors invaluable to a watercolorist.

The figure quickie is executed chiefly as an exercise, though it often results in a painting complete enough to frame and hang. Two such quickies are the paintings by Helen Batchelor (Plate 23) and Rebecca Spencer Files (Plate 24). The charm of these watercolors lies in their depiction of mood and in their convincing freedom of movement.

The quickie is useful as a preliminary for figures to be included in a sustained landscape. Because such figures are often little more than suggested, it is advisable that the painter be able to describe them in a minimum of strokes.

As a practice for fashion illustrators, it is also beneficial because it teaches one to eliminate nonessentials and to emphasize important accents.

Two brushes are sufficient, the one-inch flat sable and

a fine-pointed sable. I would suggest two jars of water, one for mixing paint and the other for cleaning the brushes. Have some clean dry cloths available for the purpose of blotting or wiping dry an overly wet area. Some painters advocate the use of paper tissues for this. The knife is useful for scraping, and the sponge, if squeezed between the fingers to form a point, may serve as a brush to apply or remove paint.

There are two quite diverse ways in which to approach the execution of a quickie. The first, method A, concerns drawing with line, then introducing the mass of color. The second, method B, involves applying the volume or area, then explaining it through the use of line.

METHOD A

1. Study the pose and balance. Do this until you can feel the swing of the pose and understand the distribution of weight.

2. Plan the general color scheme. Select for the line a color that will feature in the finished plan. If, for example, a good bit of bare skin is displayed—as in a nude or a figure in a bathing suit—a warm color may be chosen. In such a casual composition, it makes little difference that the color as well as the line of the body shows through the clothes.

3. Draw lightly the predominating action line of the pose, whether that line is actually seen or merely imagined.

4. Indicate the outline and proportions of the figure. Draw the essential lines, those necessary to describe the bulk of character of the subject. The lines may be varied as to width and may even trail off into rough brushing.

Each one, however, must be telling. The drawing should not be sketched in small strokes, but done confidently and boldly.

5. Color areas are washed over the line drawing. Be careful not simply to "fill in" as in kindergarten art. Neatness in this treatment is not a necessary factor, but crispness is. When the lines and the color areas do not quite correspond, the off-register effect sometimes produces an illusion of movement. The color areas should be introduced in broad strokes with a large brush, and the color should be determinate. This doesn't necessarily mean intense. It may be neutralized, but must be definite, indicating that the painter knows what he wants. For the sake of freshness, some artists may prefer to blend on the paper.

An area of rough brushing may serve as a ditch across which paint and water cannot flow. Borders of unpainted paper are also useful. In order to overpaint with dark, hard-edged areas, the artist should wipe or blot the area dry. He must apply color darker and more brilliant to allow for the lightening effect of blotting. The moisture of the overpainted color may blur or diffuse portions of the already painted lines. Permit this action, since it is often effective, if kept under control.

METHOD B

This approach, resembling that of calligraphy (the art of symbols superimposed on abstract color areas), is the exact reverse of the aforementioned method A. Instead of superimposing color, add the line last to describe and define the abstract areas. (Study Plates 25 and 26.)

1. Observe the pose and balance, etc.
2. Plan the color scheme, as before.

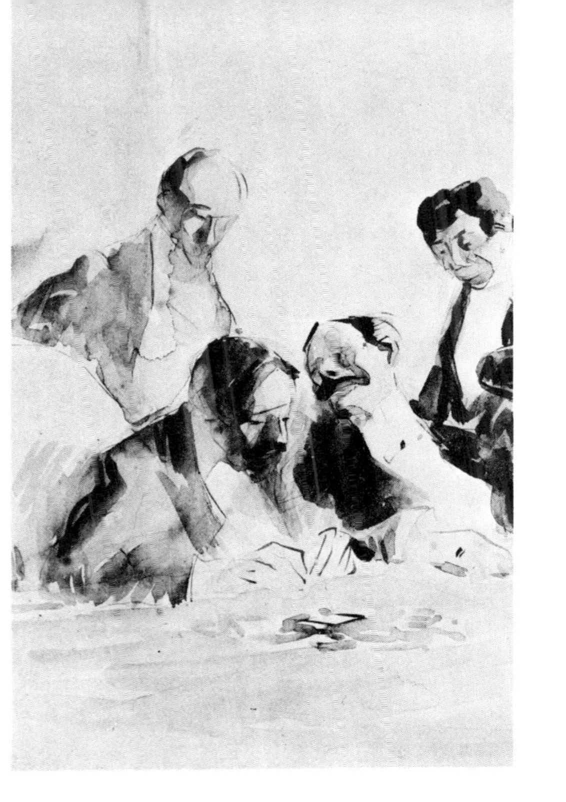

PLATE 25. Jean Louis Forain: "La Table de Jeu"—detail. Personalities revealed with an economy of wash and line. *Courtesy, Albert H. Wiggin Collection, Boston Public Library.*

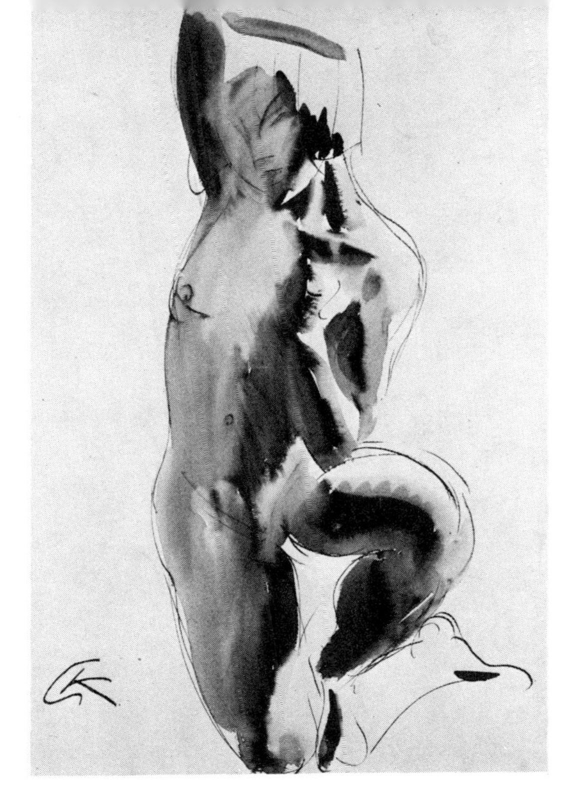

PLATE 26. George Kolbe: "Nude Study." Simplified form in the sculptor's sketch. *Courtesy, The Cleveland Museum of Art.*

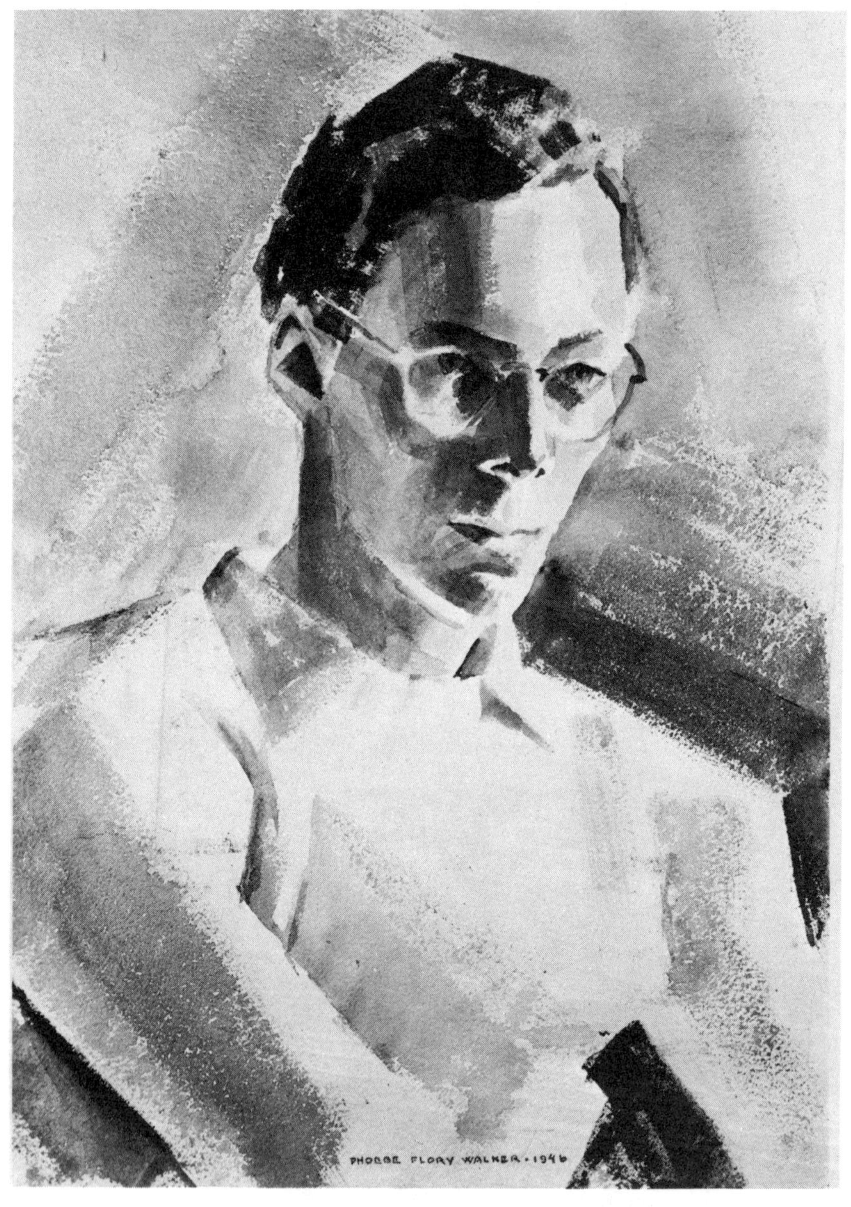

PLATE 27. Phoebe Flory: "Canadian Skier." Rough brushing permits the use of sharper angles.

3. Introduce the predominating color masses in generally accurate proportion, but with boldness. Continue to add other important areas, taking care not to infringe on the rights of line. Don't become too literal when dealing with volume, and keep the masses simple. (But guard against carelessness. The moment the painter begins to throw his paint at the "canvas," the painting becomes a failure!) The background, or suggestion of background, is introduced in the same manner.

4. This done, you are ready to explain your abstract composition by the use of line. The original areas of color need not be completely dry by the time you begin the drawing. Indeed, a certain amount of blending between area and line may be desirable. In method A you do not "fill in" the lines. By the same token, in method B you would not simply "outline" the masses. Again review in your mind the essential lines to indicate the pose, the balance of weight, and perhaps the characteristic details of the particular subject (such as curly hair, or a ruffled or pleated dress). Draw these lines in sweeping strokes, if possible, and give them as much "snap" as you can muster.

When a group works together, its members may volunteer as models. This gives everyone the opportunity to feel the various poses as well as to depict them.

The model strikes a pose and the painters seat themselves around him, not closer than ten feet. All study him for two minutes. At the end of this time, a volunteer monitor blows a whistle and the painting begins. After five minutes the whistle blows again. All artists cease work immediately. Models should be changed frequently in order to provide a variety of types, clothing, poses, and colors; then the procedure is repeated. In all, five or six positions may be held. The last sketch should show a definite improvement over the first, because the painter has, by this time, become accustomed to the pace that is required, and has loosened up and accommodated himself to the style. For the sake of variety, modify the length of the poses. Make one two minutes and another ten minutes long. Note the difference in results. The shorter one may be more sparkling, the sustained one more accurate. At the end of a session each painter should set up three of the sketches he considers his best, and the group compare and discuss them.

Should a painter work alone, he may ask a friend or a model to pose, and limit himself by strict timing. He may vary the studies by painting his subject in several different poses and a variety of clothing. The model may keep time in order that the painter may devote himself to his work.

One of the most attractive qualities of a successful quickie is its textural variety, both intentional and accidental. Because of the speed and the use of inadvertent run-ins, there is a greater risk of failure, but the advantage of spontaneity far outweighs the disadvantage of chance catastrophes.

In order to free the painter from mechanical problems and allow him to devote his entire attention to the painting, he should have an ample supply of pigment on his palette, and, close at hand, a generous supply of paper (both rough and smooth, cut into quarter sheets), plenty of rags, and at least two jars of clean water.

Having been permitted in this and the previous chapters an extensive assortment of brush strokes, you will be asked, in the next one, "The Rough-brushed Method," to limit your textures in order to become familiar with the particular advantages of that approach.

D.S.

CHAPTER XIII

THE ROUGH-BRUSHED METHOD

ONE OF THE many ways of painting a watercolor portrait is with a predominantly rough-brushed texture. This is done by using a brush that is fairly dry or held at an angle almost horizontal to the paper. Since there are no limited drying periods, some students find this method easier than techniques requiring a swifter pace.

The rough texture gives an impression of technical freshness. The color may be used more intensely, since the interspersed speckles of white paper neutralize the pigment just as much as would the addition of white paint. Two intense colors placed next to each other give a luminous effect—as the Impressionists discovered.

Since the amount of sizing on rough paper varies, in order to anticipate how the paper will behave it is best to remove the sizing entirely (by sponging and drying beforehand; some painters prefer not to pre-sponge rough paper because they like to work with the resistance of the sizing, despite the fact that it varies between packages of paper). Do *not*, however, stretch the paper, as that would rob you of the rough surface on which you rely.

Each stroke should be painted at the first shot with the correct hue and value, so clip to your board a sample sheet on which to test each brush load.

Since every brush stroke shows, do not make them all the same width. The use of different brushes or two strokes carefully joined so as not to show the seam will contribute to this variety. In the illustration, for example, "Canadian Skier" (Plate 27), the sweater and background were done entirely with a 2-inch camel hair brush. The head was painted with flat-stroke sables varying in widths from an inch and a quarter, through the one inch to the half inch, and a few details added with a fine-pointed brush. A large brush may be pinched together with the fingers to make it narrower, so that you need not be restricted by the width.

You may do the drawing in pencil if you prefer, although it is better to draw with the brush, since it is quicker and keeps you thinking in large areas.

Use any color you like mixed with considerable water: a warm color (like orange) or a cool (like blue or green), preferably not gray, since your drawing will show in the finished painting and gray would contribute nothing to the clarity of subsequent colors.

Place the head and figure, and design the principal areas of the painting with long, free brush strokes. If you misplace a line occasionally, the light pigment may be removed by blotting it up immediately with a clean rag or a squeezed-out brush.

Before you begin to paint, review the rough-brushing exercises to get used to the variety of textures available in rough brushing.

The painting may be done in sharp planes with the separate brush strokes showing, or treated in rounder forms by scumbling or blending the edges of the strokes while they are still damp.

Since the intervening speckles of white paper dilute both values and intensity, hit the colors harder than you would in a solid wash. If anything, exaggerate the value;

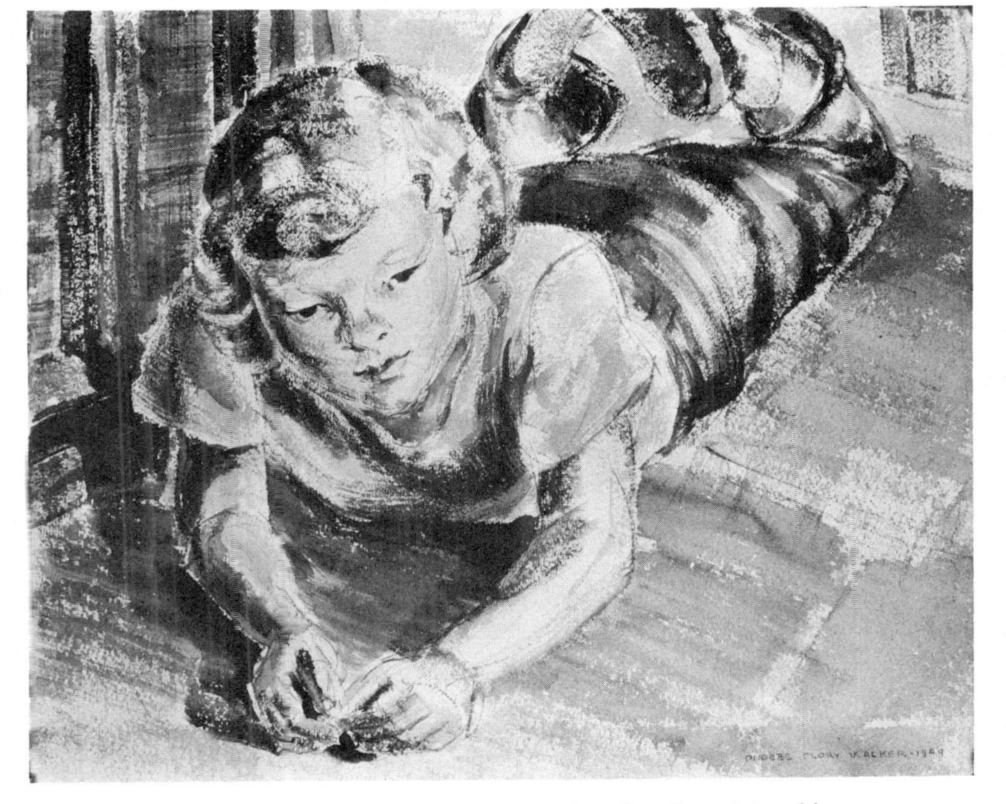

PLATE 28. Phoebe Flory: 'Listening." The unfinished quality of rough brushing can express childhood.

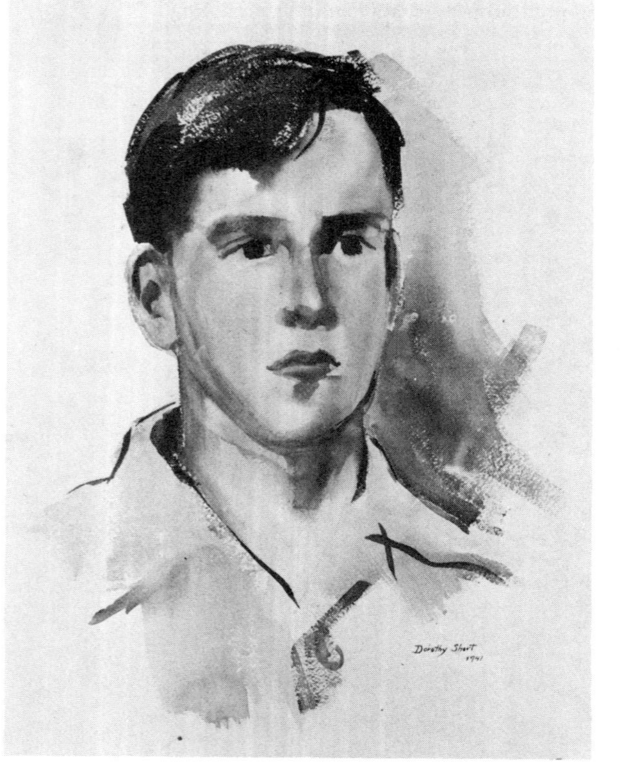

PLATE 29. Dorothy Short: "Fifteen." The inadvertent rough brushing and run-ins that occur in the quickie should be valued as part of its charm.

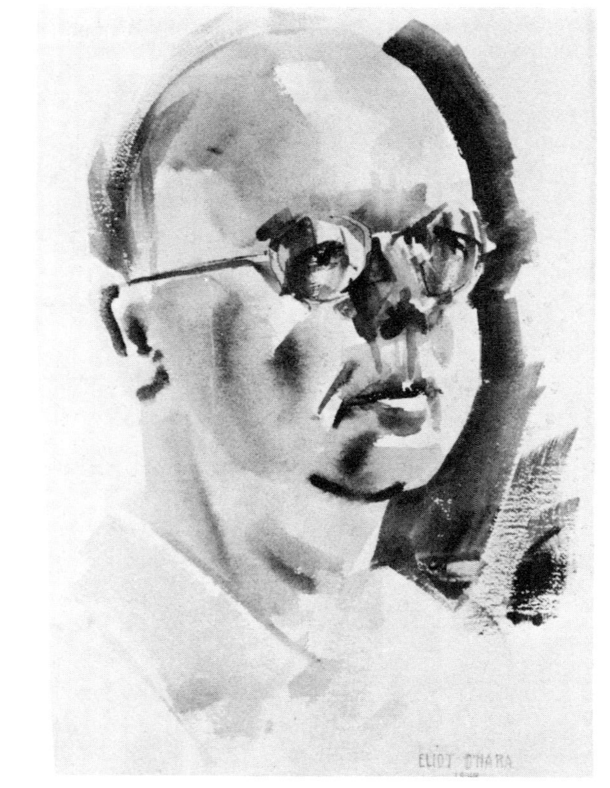

PLATE 30. Eliot O'Hara: "Harry Markley." Five-minute class demonstration for portrait quickies in black and white.

you may then remove some of the pigment by blotting it up with the side of your flat brush, without losing the rough texture.

Since each stroke is completed in one drying time, this may be called direct painting.

You may finish one section of the portrait at a time (as in the previously described method of direct painting), or you may build up the whole composition gradually, by doing all the darks first to establish the light and dark design, then the medium, and finally the light values. Still another procedure is to develop the color pattern by painting the predominant hue wherever it occurs and echoing it elsewhere, then another color, etc. This is helpful in establishing the warm and cool pattern.

Vary the degree of roughness (see "Listening," Plate 28). You may wish more white paper to show through in the lighter areas, and the shadows to be more solid; a rough texture for near or important forms and softer blended textures for less prominent ones.

Paint with the larger brushes and do not add details until you have taken a rest and viewed the painting from a distance. This is even more important in rough brushing than in other techniques, as distance seems to fuse the strokes and to reduce the roughness.

Since there are no drying times to consider, you may take as much or as little time as you desire, but if you return to this technique after studying the next chapter on "Quickies" you will notice a decided improvement.

P.F.

CHAPTER XIV

PORTRAIT QUICKIES

A QUICKIE portrait helps one to form the good habits of making on-the-spot decisions, of working fast, and of eliminating nonessential details. As a loosening-up exercise, it is useful immediately before a portrait done in a more studied style, or even during the painting, if the artist feels himself becoming tense. The rigid discipline of timed quickies for speeding one's pace is invaluable.

The spontaneity of the approach is responsible for the freshness and brilliancy found in most quickies. The painter is more concerned with the pattern of large areas and a dramatic, sparkling effect than with extravagant detail. Because of the necessity for speed, there is a greater chance to profit by "happy accidents," opportune run-ins, and unpredicted textures. Unlike the other methods, in which the model must hold a lengthy pose, the quickie sitting time is often ten to twenty minutes. This permits a more natural position and one involving more action. The pose should be continuous, if possible, with no rests.

The palette should be clean and well supplied with moist pigment. In addition to the usual equipment, the artist should also provide himself with a stock of clean rags for wiping dry certain areas that he may desire light in value, or adjacent to which he wishes a hard line or a rough-brushed area. Due to the required speed, he cannot allow time to wait for a natural drying. The paper may be almost any kind that will take watercolor. Even a lightweight paper is suitable, for the pace of the painting will prevent warping during the process. The knife may prove a useful tool for dividing a wet area into two parts, to avert their flowing together, or to accent a dark.

The preliminary contemplation of the model should occupy as much time as the painting itself. There should be no pencil drawing. If the painter feels the need of some guide, however, a thin, light line, drawn with a fine brush, is suggested to indicate placement and proportion of the figure and features. The less drawing, the more spontaneous the painting.

It is preferable for the artist to start by blocking in areas, making the division between them serve as outlines. If the light on the model is at all strong, the portions in direct light may be left pure white paper. The shadows, then, must describe the form.

Because of the limited time allowed, and because of the casual nature of the quickie portrait, a vignetted background is often appropriate when this method is used for a finished work. It should be painted with an eye to keying the colors—that is, emphasizing a color by surrounding it with its complement—and intensifying, by contrast, the lights and darks in the face. The portrait, "Fifteen" (Plate 29), is an impression of the boy, done in about twenty minutes, in a very fluid style. The limited background serves merely to contrast with the face, and to suggest space around the head.

Since there is little time for conscious decisions, the artist's previously formed habits come almost automatically into play. Anything he has learned on surface textures (Chapter X), for example, serves to enrich the quickie. In Eliot O'Hara's five-minute portrait,

"Harry Markley" (Plate 30), the double-loaded brush helped to model the planes of the cheek, neck, etc.; whisking strokes described the hair; rough brushing suggested the shirt, background, and glint of light on the glasses; and the knife indicated the rim of the glasses.

A quickie also is excellent as a preliminary color sketch for a portrait in a more sustained style. By painting a series of identical heads with different-colored backgrounds, one may determine the most pleasing and interesting combination.

As a portrait itself, it may be a charming and telling comment, for often a quickie achieves the most accurate portrayal of character and a fleeting expression.

Wet blending requires the same deft and rapid handling as the quickie; so, with this method still fresh in your mind, and dexterity in your finger tips, turn to the chapter that follows.

D.S.

CHAPTER XV

WET BLENDING

Wet blending is a term used to indicate the fusing or flowing of paint through an area so thoroughly dampened as to prevent the possibility of any hard edges, and to achieve a soft, fluid effect.

It is, perhaps, the most typical treatment within the medium of watercolor because it avails itself to the greatest extent of the flowing, impressionistic quality that has often characterized that medium. This quality is admirably exhibited in "Rotisserie," by George Grosz (Plates 32 and 17).

In many ways, it is the most difficult to handle, because the element of speed, the judgment concerning the relative amount of pigment and water required, and the necessity for immediate decisions are all of paramount importance.

This style is especially suited to children's portraits, because it is fast and direct. Speed is the most important factor in the painting of children. This swifter process gives one the chance to study the child in motion, but requires comparatively little time for the actual working of the brush on paper. Thus, it helps prevent the unfortunate "studied" look that sometimes deprives a child's portrait of the necessary and characteristic freshness.

Timing in the wet-blended method differs from that in all other styles. When the entire painting is to be accomplished in one drying period, there must be no interruption after the paper is once dampened and the paint applied.

The drawing may take as long as you wish, and may include one or more rest periods. The simplest rendering, however, is best. Mere direction lines are all that are necessary. Indeed, a more complicated drawing is useless, since, in this particular method, one's precarious control over the flowing of paint does not permit too great a precision of line. Should a group work without instruction, it is advisable to appoint a monitor to call time, so that all members may begin working simultaneously.

The materials used in this method include the usual set of equipment, plus one or more of the artificial aids for prolonging drying. These are numerous:

1. Glucose—a heavy sugar syrup, which, when dissolved in water (approximately two teaspoons to a glass) extends the drying period one-half again as long. Warning should be given here concerning the handicaps of this practice. The glucose has a tendency to seal in pencil lines so that they cannot be removed later. It also fixes the paint to the paper, making wipe-outs difficult, if not impossible. If these handicaps are understood and allowances made (by limiting the number and intensity of pencil lines, and by *not* relying on wipe-outs), this practice will prove satisfactory. When, however, the watercolor is to hang in a tropical or humid climate, glucose, like the old-fashioned pigments in which honey was used as a binder, encourages mildew.

2. Glycerin—which may be added in the amount of one or two drops to a glass of water—will prolong the drying time and permit the painter to work with more deliberation.

3. The use of a saturated blotter, placed beneath the paper on the board, will keep it evenly wet for a longer period than the glucose, but will, consequently, hamper the accents of sharper edges, which may be added during the various stages, short of dry. Some painters back their paper with blankets and newspapers to retain the moisture. Some advocate the use of a fixative blower to spray a fine mist (of water, or of water and glycerin) on the surface without disturbing the already applied paint. Others prefer the practice of soaking the paper beforehand.

4. One may also use the weather to advantage by selecting a rainy or humid day for a wet-blended portrait. If some arrangement may be made to supplement the reduced intensity of light, damp weather is to be preferred. The drying time is automatically lengthened, and you may work more easily without undue haste. Any dry heat in the room, however, will cancel this advantage.

The paper best adapted to wet blending is a heavy, rough rag (140–300 lb.) because it will hold moisture without buckling, and will not dry with too sharp edges. A smooth paper may be used, but it requires an even more accelerated speed. Certain smooth papers absorb paint so completely that it is impossible to remove or lighten it after it is applied. Therefore, it is best to test each new kind before taking a chance. The staining colors, of course, may not be completely removed after application, regardless of whether paper is wet or dry.

In executing a wet-blended portrait, it is imperative that the artist assign a certain amount of time to a thorough study of the arrangement, and to planning the color scheme and composition, until he can visualize the finished work. He will find it helpful to make a series of color and value samples, in order to simplify the color combinations and to determine his choice. He may also wish to experiment with the effect of pigment introduced into a saturated area, to discover the degree of fading in drying. Most important of all, he must definitely fix in his mind his intention, know exactly what he wants to express, and what he considers most noteworthy about each particular setup. He must know which traits he wishes to exaggerate or distort, and which ones he wishes to subordinate. (See Chapter XVIII on "Intention.") In wet blending there is no opportunity during the painting to stand back and appraise one's progress.

The composition planned, one may proceed toward the actual painting. The materials are arranged (on a table, if possible), the board tilted slightly toward the artist, and the palette, clean and freshly supplied with paint, is placed within reach. One may use the one-inch and one-half-inch flat brushes, and a fine, pointed sable, plus the two-inch, for covering large areas rapidly.

Before beginning the portrait, certain exercises are recommended for the purpose of achieving facility. Take a large sheet of paper, place it horizontally on your board, and divide it into five sections by lines running vertically. Then draw a series of lines across the paper, dividing it horizontally into about five squares. In the center column paint a value scale, beginning with white and ending with black. Try to keep the various steps as evenly graded as possible, but with sharp edges. This done, sponge the column to the left of center and, while it is wet, introduce paint and try to reproduce, as closely as you can, the original value scale, but with blended edges. (You may be surprised at the resulting lightness of value when the paper is dry.) After this is done, turn to the right portion and do the same, using two columns at once, since values

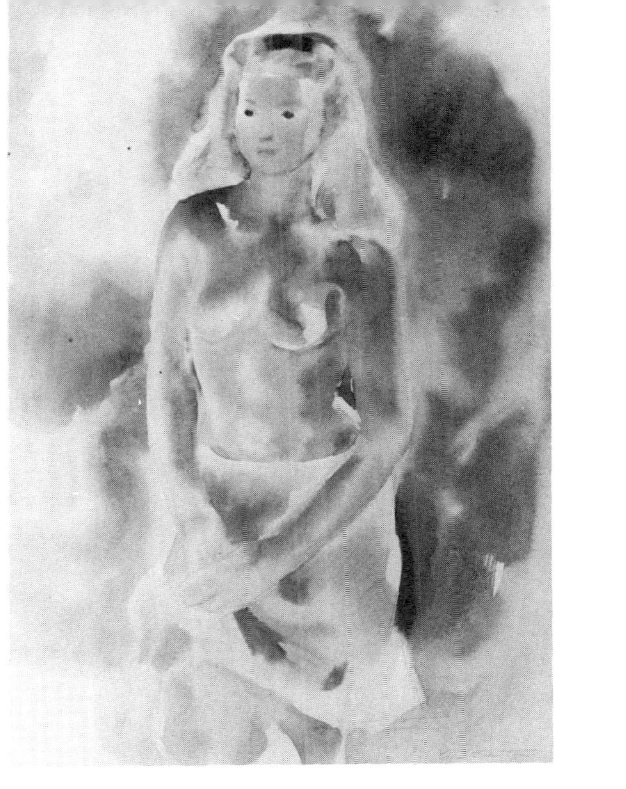

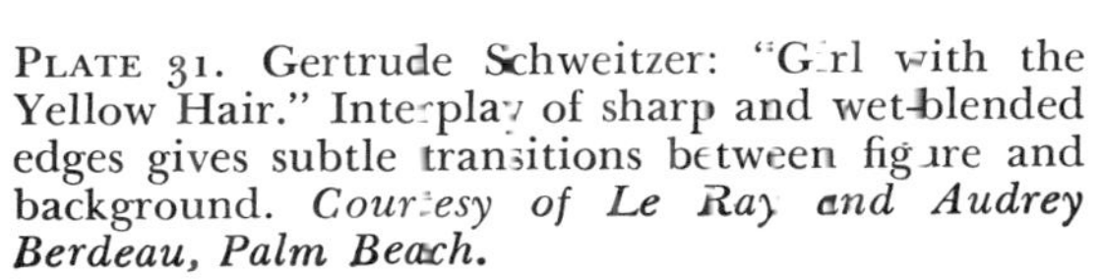

PLATE 31. Gertrude Schweitzer: "Girl with the Yellow Hair." Interplay of sharp and wet-blended edges gives subtle transitions between figure and background. *Courtesy of Le Ray and Audrey Berdeau, Palm Beach.*

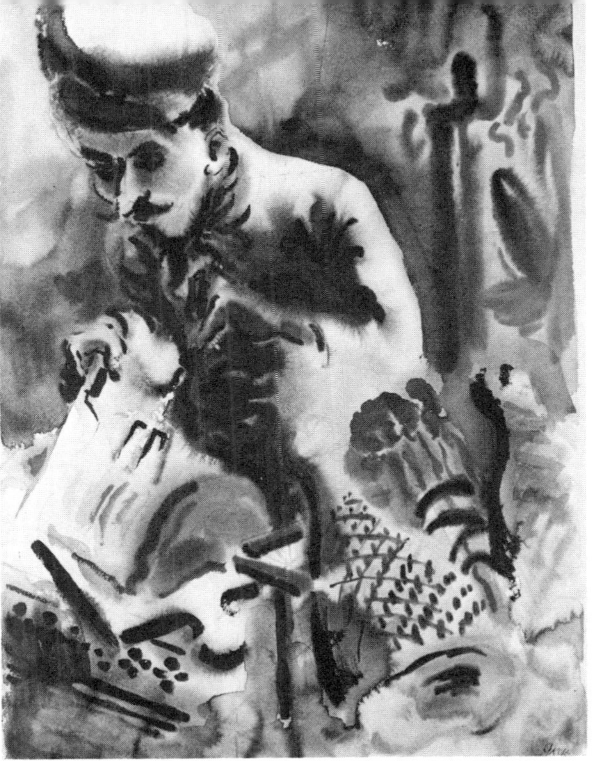

PLATE 32. George Grosz: "Rotisserie." A wealth of textures within the bounds of wet blending. *Courtesy, Mrs. Solomon Diamond. Photograph courtesy Associated American Artists Galleries.*

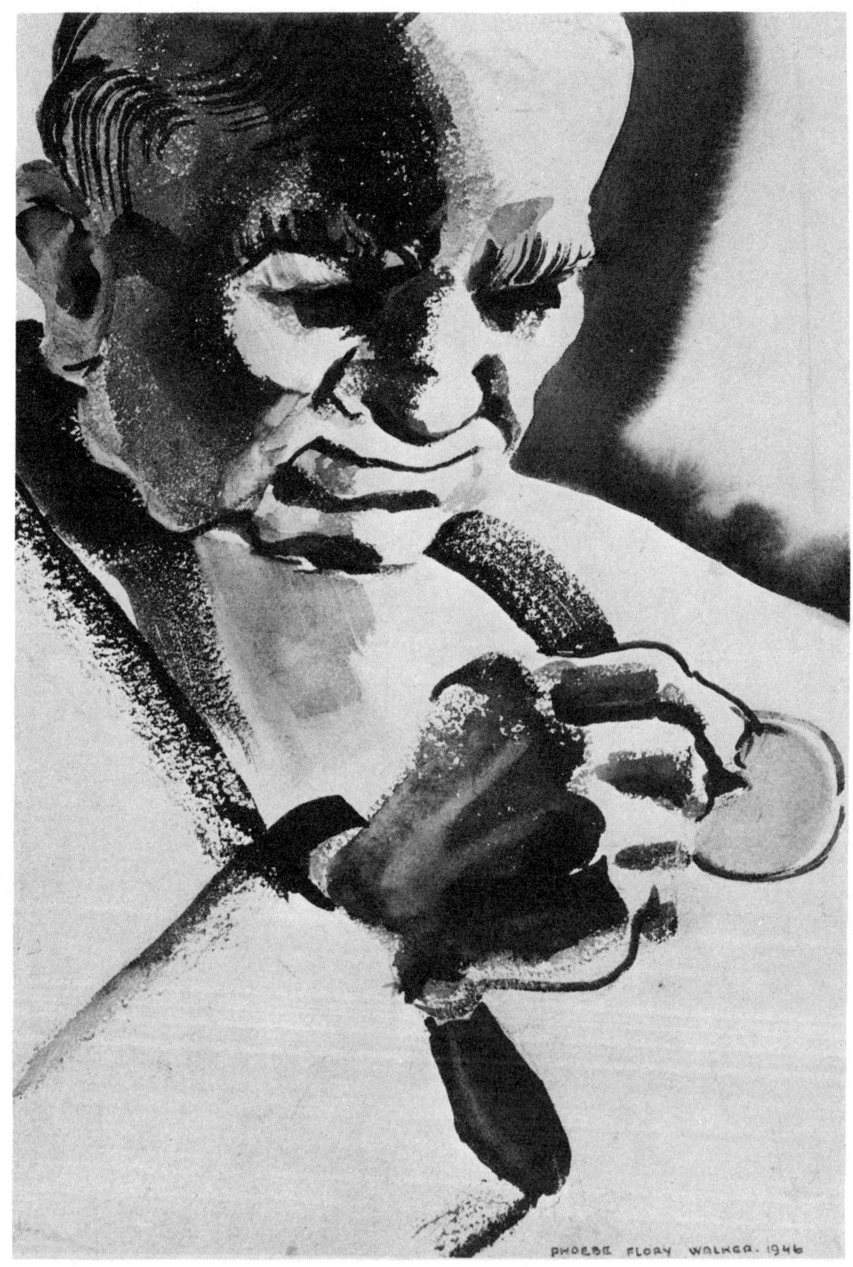

PLATE 33. Phoebe Flory: "These Dimming Eyes." White-paper intervals prevent clashes among bright colors as well as among textures.

tend to fade even more in larger areas. Paint another strip and practice different degrees of blending, as the paper passes through the various stages from wet to dry.

Having become somewhat familiar with the characteristics and problems of wet blending, turn to your portrait and the setup at hand. The composition may be indicated by a minimum of lines. Only enough are needed to suggest the position of the head, its relation to the neck, and the slant of the shoulders. If the background is to have any strong design, the general movement may be suggested. Lines denoting placement of the features and their approximate proportion are sufficient within the outline of the head.

After the drawing is completed the paper should be saturated. This may be done by a large brush or sponge, as in any other wash. The surplus water is flowed off in order to prevent puddles in the center and balloons around the edge of the paper. There must be just enough moisture to permit the flow of paint without the loss of control. Color should be introduced much *darker* than in an ordinary wash, and *dryer,* because the water already on the paper will dilute it. A certain amount of diffusion results and contributes to the fluid effect. One must take care, at the same time, not to drown in it. Should less diffusion be desired, the artist may allow the surface to dry slightly before introducing the paint. The painting by George Grosz (Plates 32 and 17) illustrates the use of the various drying stages for different effects. As soon as the surface begins to lose its sheen, work should stop immediately. When the paper is half dry, a brush, damp or dry, will remove color. The painter must wait until the surface is bone dry, so that a flow of water won't disturb the particles of pigment already on the paper; then he may resaturate the entire sheet and continue.

There are occasions, however, when one may intentionally take off color. The use of wipe-outs (the removing of paint and water from a saturated area with a dry brush) constitutes another means of achieving effect in this method. As in applying water and paint, the removing of them requires practice for proficiency. A wipe-out must be made when the paper is at just the right stage of dampness for each of the various results. If the artist wishes merely to lighten the area in general, he may remove color and water when the surface is saturated. But if he wishes a stroke to show, he will wait until the surface is just beginning to lose its sheen before wiping out, with a large brush for broad areas, and, for accents, a small one or a large flat brush, especially a short-haired one, pinched to a chisel-like edge. In the strictly wet-blended process, no wipe-outs should be made after the paper is dry. This is especially true on smooth paper, because such wipe-outs tend to be sharper than on rough.

If one wishes to wet blend a portrait at more leisure, one may divide the area into sections and dampen each of these as one comes to it, joining adjacent areas by resaturating and overlapping. (See Chapter VI, "Modeling with Paint.") As a modification of the wet-blended technique, edges of some sections may be left intentionally, as in Gertrude Schweitzer's "Girl with the Yellow Hair" (Plate 31).

Though wet blending is one of the most difficult methods, the artist will find that it will become increasingly more workable with each attempt. Once his confidence is established, half the battle is won.

D.S.

CHAPTER XVI

SELECTIVE COLOR

FROM a consideration of blending colors and values, we now turn to a more complex problem, that of choosing them.

Almost no watercolor painting that is a representation of nature finds acceptance in contemporary exhibitions. A close approach to realism is now often merely one of the exercises for learning techniques, like scales and arpeggios in music. [How tastes do change! This statement, so true when this book was first published in 1949, no longer holds. It would appear that realism, in its many and varied forms, is back with a vengeance—one of the reasons that we feel it important to republish this book. P.F.]

An exact representation of nature is not necessary. The fact that such an infinite variety of values, hues, intensity, and surface textures exists in nature is no reason for our using them all in one picture. To do so would be like going to a delicatessen and eating a sample of everything there. When painting "from nature," the artist's taste is sufficient reason for him to change her colors, or to select the ones he likes from her store of riches.

"Selective color," by the way, is treated here not in the sense of its being a combination chosen to describe the artist's or his subject's personality, or the painter's reaction to his subject. Here we mean its selection more for decorative than for interpretative purposes, to achieve a desired quality in a picture. It isn't possible, however, wholly to divorce a choice of colors for decoration from a choice for interpretation, and both processes are subjective with the painter.

To begin an experiment with selection, you may start out with one color, or a relationship between two, probably choosing something that appeals to you in the portrait subject or his surroundings. Let it be important in its position on the paper and interesting in its shape and dimensions, since it was this color that first attracted you as a starting point in this particular design. The pale blue eyes and tanned skin were Phoebe Flory's starting point in "Girl in Plaid" (Plate 34).

For such a preliminary sampling of color you could use rectangles of different shapes and sizes, or circles in a neutral gray background. This would permit you to concentrate a little less on pattern and to keep the work in the realm of pure color. The pattern, it is true, must always intrude, and any black or gray intervals between areas are a part of the design.

Now try a second color in your arrangement. After putting it on, make it a little lighter or a little darker—which is better? Next, vary the hue within the same value. That is, move it clockwise or counterclockwise around the spectrum circle. Go past the exact point each way, as you would focus binoculars from either side of just right, or as a violinist would tune his E string to its proper relationship with A. In the illustration (Plate 34), the model's gray dress gave the artist a wide latitude for selective color.

Here you have an approach to subjective painting. There is still a question of preference in the matter of intensity. How brilliant or how gray should each color be?

You are now ready to risk a third color and smaller

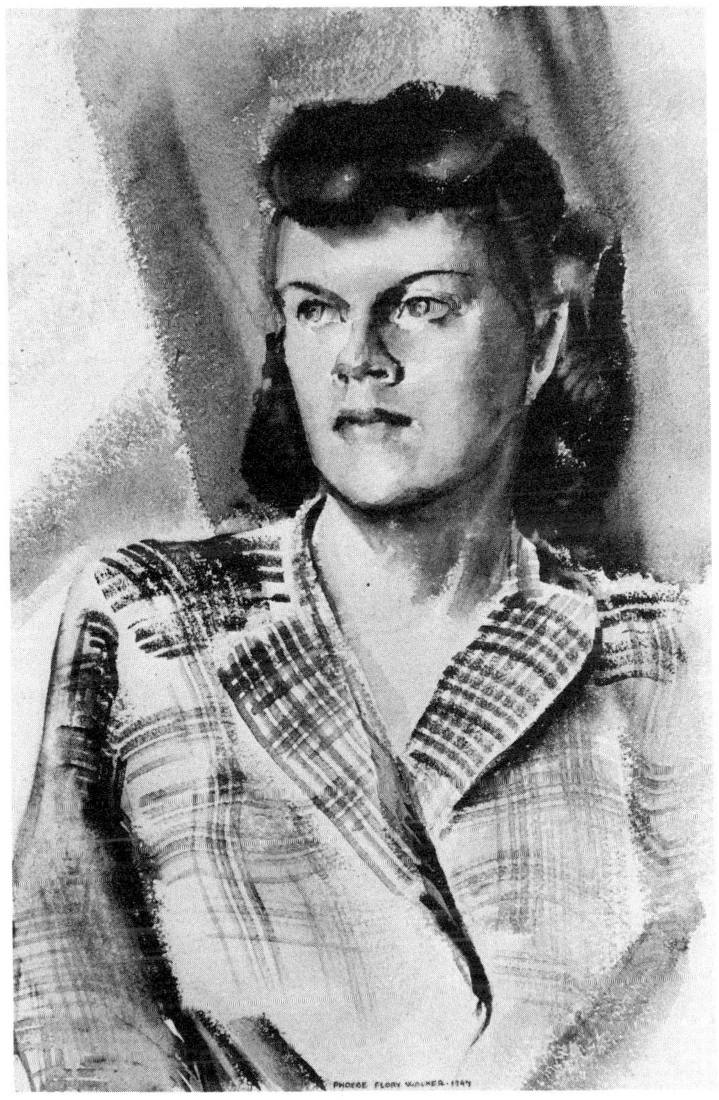

PLATE 34. Phoebe Flory: "Girl in Plaid." While other colors might have been included, combinations of blue and orange were purposely selected. (Reproduced in color on the back cover.)

echoes of the first two in different parts of the paper. While the size or position of these spots or areas will be determined more by instinct than by any preconceived plan, in any color arrangement, quantity, or the relative size of the areas, can make or break the picture.

By trial and error you proceed to develop the theme set for you by your earlier choosings. Make advances and retreats in the value and brilliance of each new ingredient until it satisfies you in its relationship with what is already on the paper.

The wisdom of adding a fourth hue is doubtful. The more notes you include, the more easily will you produce a discord. (Not that a color dissonance is always a false note; sometimes it is more effective than harmony. Your taste will guide you as to when you should be startled or repelled by what is on the paper.) Try then, by covering this or that spot with your hand, to discover which is the offending element. It may not be the last one you put on. The moment, therefore, that you experience a pleasant reaction from your painting—emotional rather than intellectual—is a good time to stop and appraise your results.

If you add anything from now on it should be only repeats of values and colors that are already on the paper, or a completion of the design by filling in the blanks with gray. These grays may be slightly flavored with any of the elements of the harmony.

This way of creating an abstract color plan is offered, of course, not because it produces a work of art in itself, but as a stimulus to the instinctive perceptions that help to govern the choice of colors for our portrait. Now that your selection of sample colors is completed, you may apply these hues in approximately the same quantities to painting an actual portrait.

From the beginnings of art, color has been "selected," both for its own sake and to enhance interpretation. One thinks of Van Gogh and many other painters with an especially sensitive response to the possibilities of color.

Certain artists like to surround or divide color areas with heavy lines—Georges Rouault, Max Weber, and Abraham Rattner, for instance. Such dark intervals, of course, resemble nothing in nature, but serve to emphasize relationships of space and hue. The result then consists of spots of selected colors arranged to balance in depth and size. Other artists separate them by white paper, as will be described in the next chapter.

It is assumed that our present distortion of nature's colors is chiefly for decorative purposes. The same preliminary method of an abstract exercise, however, may be adapted to other assignments. Return to it later to enrich your portraits.

E.O'H.

CHAPTER XVII

WHITE-PAPER INTERVALS

In a white-paper portrait, carefully selected colors are surrounded by large areas of white in such a way as to suggest that the color extends also into the unpainted paper. The Japanese frequently paint a sky with a strip of blue at the top fading down to nothing, and we assume without effort that the blue sky continues to the horizon.

In a white-paper portrait, as much as 75 per cent of the paper may be untouched by pigment. A completely painted head with a background vignetted off to white is not a white-paper picture. It is a realistic portrait with a large white mat. The color areas as well as the uncolored ones should be designed to the edges of the composition, and unpainted intervals distributed throughout.

The shapes and quantities of the intervals are as significant as the painted areas they surround, just as the spacing and length of the rests in music are as important as the notes themselves.

Such a picture, painted with selection and restraint, may be a powerfully suggestive interpretation, with chosen characteristics emphasized and the rest understated; or it may be treated as a decorative portrait, where the design both of the color areas and of the white-paper intervals is as important as the identity of the subject. In either case it can be a likeness, and may be done from a model or from sketches of a model (see Chapter XXIV) or from one of your previously painted realistic portraits.

The white-paper picture may be light in tone or sharply contrasting. Remember, if you wish an emphatic portrait, however, that since the surrounding white paper tends to dilute the color you do use, you can afford to hit the values and color intensity harder than you would in a realistic picture. Where a statement begins emphatically the imagination completes it in the same vein. When you hear someone exclaim, "You great big ———," your mind fills in the blank as forcefully as your vocabulary permits.

Although some charming white-paper portraits have been painted intentionally in light values, even more often the light picture is the inadvertent result of the color being diluted by the surrounding paper. In that case it is not "charming" but merely anemic.

It is more difficult to write a short article than a long one, or to say in a few words what you would like to discuss for hours. The wealth of ideas must be distilled to its essence. In the same way a white-paper portrait requires far more preliminary planning than a realistic one, although the actual painting time is usually less.

Begin this problem by doing a sketch of the subject in solid black and solid white areas without shading, as if you were cutting a linoleum block print. Consider only how much you will say and what you will leave unsaid, and the design of the painted areas in relation to the shapes and quantity of the unpainted ones.

Omit in this first exercise all broken textures such as those produced by rough brushing and the divided-hair strokes, since they give a medium value effect just as does a diluted wash. Your black areas will all have hard edges. Although later, in your finished picture, you may use transitions of medium values, the stronger dark and light pattern will have been designed in this preliminary sketch.

When you are satisfied as to the distribution of the dark and light areas, you may go on to consider the other factors—value, color, and texture—either in penciled notes on your first sketch or in a series of quickies.

Plan first the values and textures: which of the painted areas will be the darkest and which will be in the middle value range? Where will you keep a sharp edge and where a transition graded from dark to white paper? A color that stops abruptly implies that the form it describes also stops abruptly, or else that it is overlapped by the sharp edge of a much lighter form. But if it fades off gradually the imagination infers that the color extends beyond that which is actually painted. It is, in other words, an understatement to be filled out by the observer's imagination.

Secondly, plan the colors. Since color is used in such small spots, it must be all the more carefully selected as to hue and intensity. Use only colors that express your subject, or that combine to give a decorative effect. To achieve emphatic color, you may exaggerate the intensity, just as you can the values, more than in a realistic picture. An anchovy paste hors d'oeuvre and a strawberry meringue dessert may both, if separated by the main course, contribute to a royal feast, but would be distasteful if mixed together in the same salad. So also, an intense color separated by white paper from another intense color will not clash as the two might if placed next to each other.

In any picture, when we arbitrarily limit one of the dimensions of painting, we must rely all the more heavily on the others. In the black and white portraits, since we were denied the use of color, we had to stress, in the arrangement of the masses, the differences between values, and seek added interest in textures. When we limited the textures, in the wet-blended or rough-brushed watercolor portraits, we relied more heavily on values and color. In this lesson, likewise, since we are restricting the amount of painted areas, we must place more reliance on values, colors, and textures and their distribution. In Plate 33, "These Dimming Eyes," for example, the range of textures includes wet blending, graded wash, rough brushing, whisking, and divided-hair strokes. One may combine in one white-paper portrait more tricks of texture than in most other kinds of painting. This type of picture may, in fact, be primarily an experience in textures, in which each carefully planned area creates a different but interesting tactile sensation. (The original sketch for "These Dimming Eyes" is reproduced as Plate 50.)

After you have executed a white-paper picture, is it not evident that careful planning of a portrait—or stating one's intention beforehand—would be equally helpful for other styles of painting?

P.F.

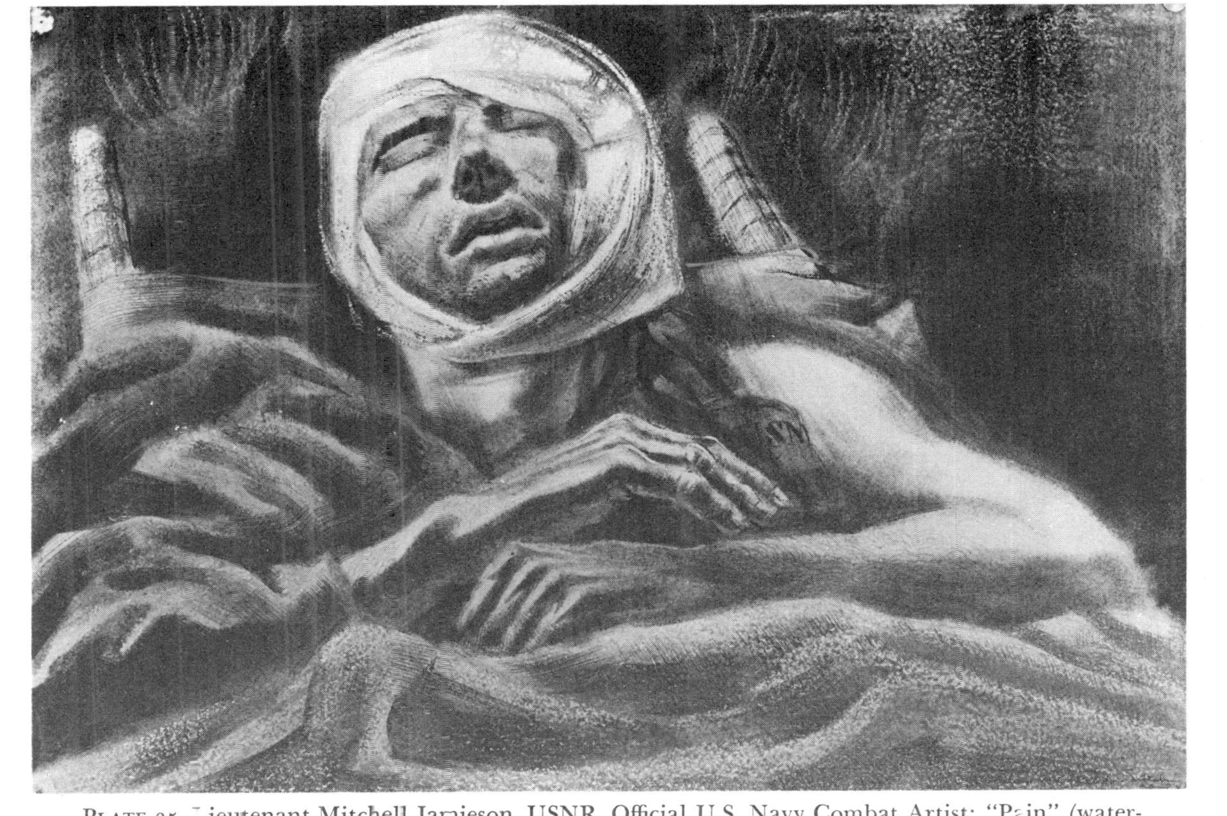

PLATE 35. Lieutenant Mitchell Jamieson, USNR, Official U.S. Navy Combat Artist: "Pain" (watercolor, ink, and crayon). Everything in the picture helps to intensify the focus on the single idea of pain. *Courtesy, United States Navy.*

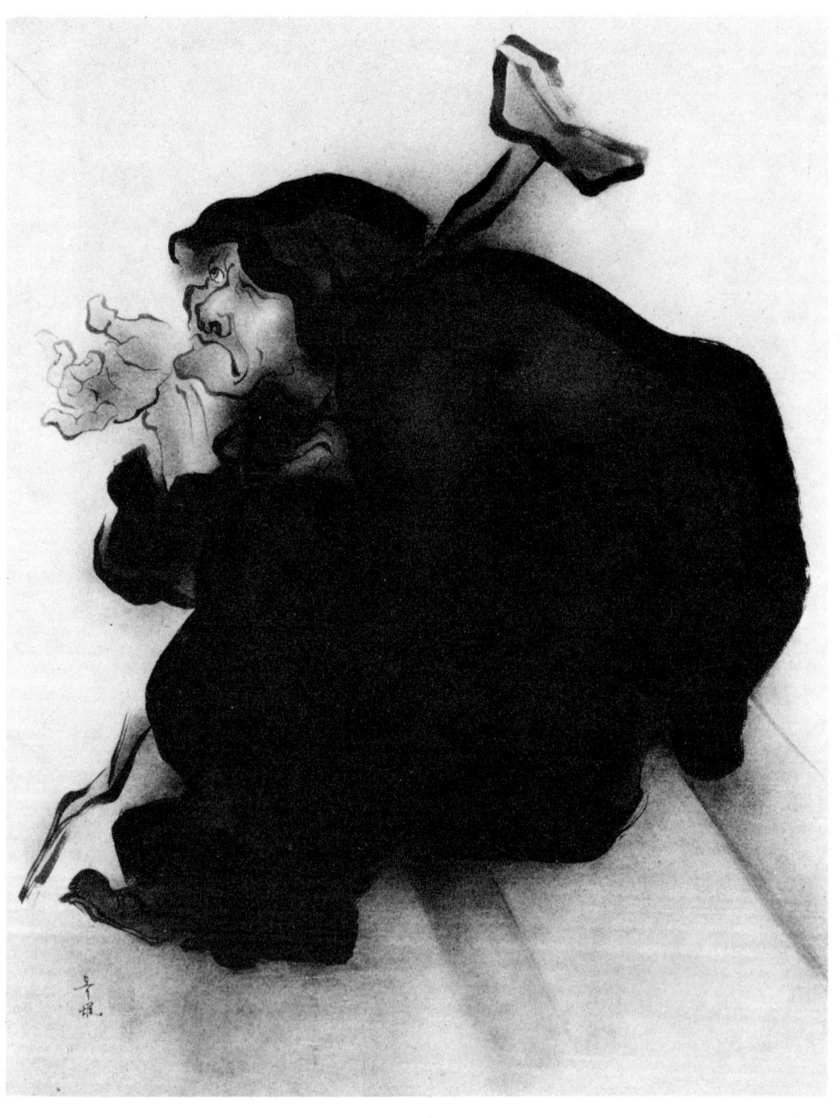

PLATE 36. Tyrus Wong: "The Beggar." Intention enables the artist to eliminate all but the essential.

CHAPTER XVIII

INTENTION

INTENTION may be defined as the reason for the choice of a subject and for the manner of painting it. The method for conducting this lesson was originally conceived by Eleanor E. Barry, of Boston, and is here adapted to portraiture. Applied to depicting people, intention means the way in which you propose to interpret the sitter. This must be determined in advance so that the entire treatment of the picture may carry it out—the pose, placement, lighting, and technique—and is the one element, more than any other, that differentiates painting from photography.

Mitchell Jamieson's watercolor, "Pain" (Plate 35), was painted from pencil sketches made on Okinawa of a Sixth Division Marine, while the stretcher bearers stopped to rest on the way to the Battalion aid station. Interpreting this picture, the artist writes:

> The dark journey, all of it, is a pain-racked nightmare to the wounded man, indistinguishable as to time or place and marked only by the high red plateaus and deep black wells of suffering.

Of his painting, "The Beggar" (Plate 36), Tyrus Wong says:

> In "The Beggar" my intention was to express the feeling and interesting character of this Mexican woman; not a

striking likeness but those features indicative of personality and to do it with simplicity and the simple palette without distracting, unnecessary elaboration.

On the general philosophy of contemplation before painting, Mr. Wong writes:

An artist may spend 30 days more or less on a painting out of which a few minutes may be actual execution time. The rest is thinking or if you wish contemplation. But before this period of constructive thinking, it is presupposed a background of technical and mental training, and for the Chinese painter a knowledge and practice of the 6 steps which are the foundation of Oriental painting. These steps are not theoretical but fundamental. They are loosely, rhythmical vitality, anatomy and brushwork, form, color, composition-space-balance, and study of classical tradition. All are self-explanatory except possibly rhythmical vitality. To me it means dynamic spirit or inspiration which links the spiritual and material and is the end result of mental preparation. It is the thing that marks the difference between the technician and the artist.

By mental training, I mean memory and observation. They are extremely important essentials. Observation and study serve to stimulate the imagination and act as visual suggestions. For instance if one planned to paint a specific subject there should be a period of close patient observation and memorizing of what is seen—possibly some preliminary sketches as a sort of artist's shorthand. The memory rejects what has not interested or impressed it and the artist is not tempted to transcribe superfluous detail. Memory and observation are merely the superficial leads to thinking. The image of something contemplated in the mind can be immediately transferred to paper with warmth. Swiftness is possible and indispensable.

The purpose of thinking is a means to a more subjective approach—of looking at life from the outside and seeing through it; yet being able to identify self with it. Possibly it is the feeling one gets when looking through the Mt. Palomar "giant eye" telescope at the universe spread out before us. When one does that—man's place in the world is insignificant, and his foibles ridiculous against the largeness of space and time. When one has understood this point, it is hoped that an awareness and sympathy for mankind coupled with humor are attained.

For this lesson it is best that you know your model or something about him before you begin. If, however, you have not met him before, allow yourself some extra time, and tell him that you want to make a series of preliminary sketches in informal poses.

When you have some idea of the interpretation you wish to convey, write out your analysis on a slip of paper, but without letting the model know what it is, for he would become self-conscious.

Your written intention will be divided into two parts: first, the dominating characteristic or the mood; second, the means by which you propose to carry it out. When you finish your picture, clip this paper to it.

Do not attempt to write an elaborate essay, for if you do, you will expend all your creative energies in words. That is just as bad for the painter as it is for an author who tells so many people all about the novel he intends to write that he never actually gets around to writing it.

And do not try to be too specific, but list only the one or perhaps two dominating qualities, since, as you paint, the characterization will emerge more clearly in your mind, and you will not have committed yourself too specifically beforehand. The intention, for example, for

"These Dimming Eyes" (Plate 33) was to convey "the physical and mental" tension of concentration. Strong value contrast, variety of textures, intense color, relieved by white-paper intervals."

In a class, if the model is not a stranger, the group may pool impressions of him before he arrives. The sitter will appear different to each person, who should draw his own conclusions.

The painting surface you select, its shape and size, as well as the figure placement, composition, colors, textures, and the general style—realistic, distorted, or abstract—all these are governed by intention.

Follow this portrait immediately with a second one of an entirely different kind of person. This should, of course, be handled in a new manner.

When you have finished both, compare them to see that you have carried out your intention and have adapted your style to suit the subject. One of your portraits may have been done in a very realistic manner, while the other may be stylized or abstract; one may have been based on linear or tactile drawing, the other stressing planes.

It is necessary to caution the student against painting the picture first and then describing the result afterward. To do that is to miss the whole point of the lesson, and is as unnecessary as showing the menu at the end of a meal.

Many professional portrait painters continue this practice of brief analyses of intention, either noted down preliminary to painting or merely kept in their minds. We have asked you this time to write it out in order to force you to make the decisions ahead of time on *what* you intend to convey, and *how* you intend to convey it.

Most painters arrive at their understanding of a person more through intuition than through conscious verbal

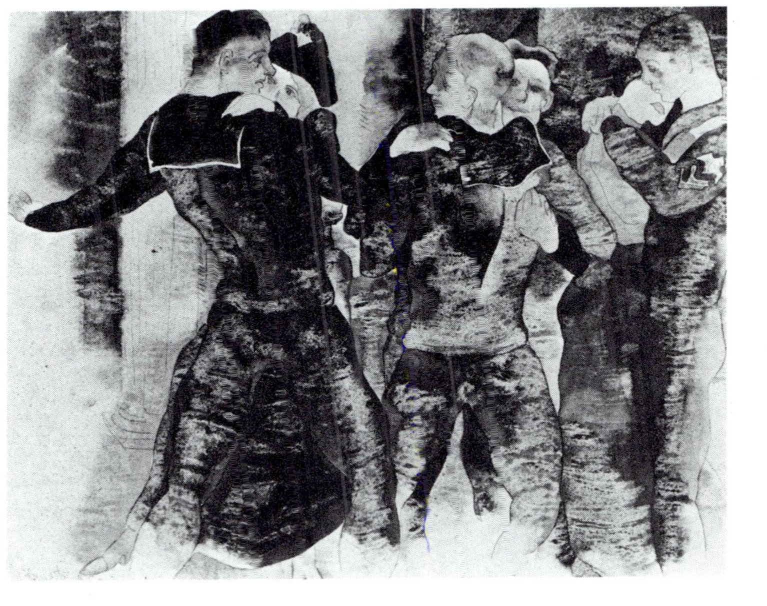

PLATE 37. Charles Demuth: "Dancing Sailors." Rough textures are possible on smooth paper. *Collection Museum of Modern Art, New York.*

PLATE 38. George Biddle: "Emporium." Smooth paper adapts itself to effective use of sharp and soft edges. *Courtesy, Whitney Museum of American Art.*

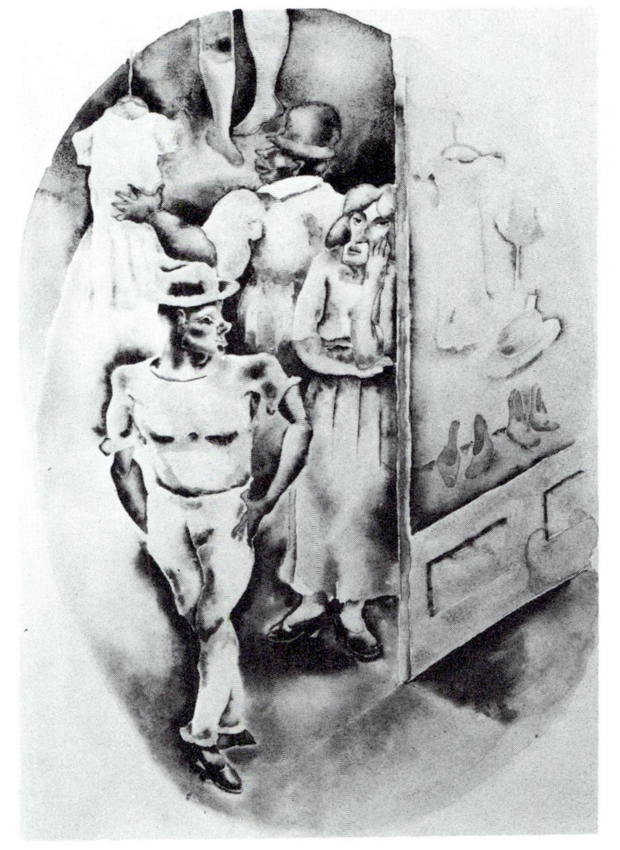

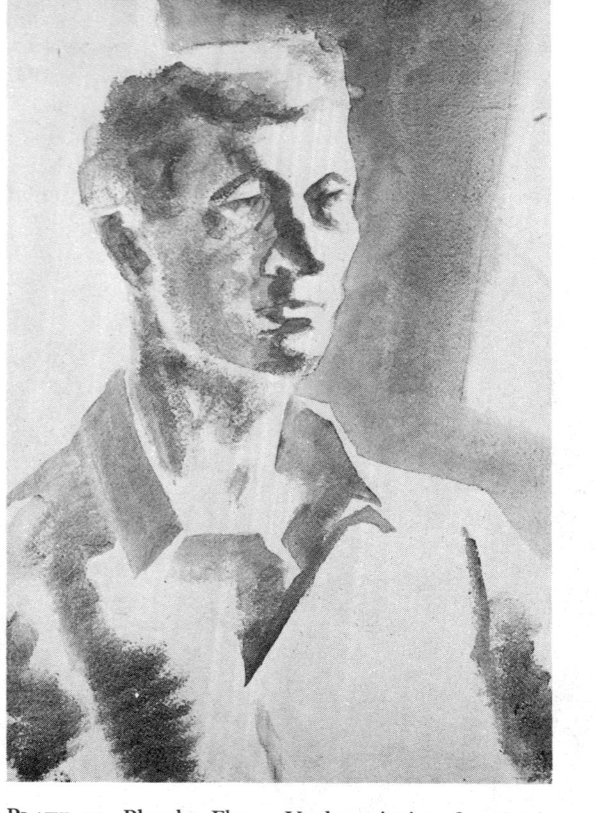

PLATE 39. Phoebe Flory: Underpainting for "Malcolm Ross." The underpainting is used in areas that will be of medium and dark values.

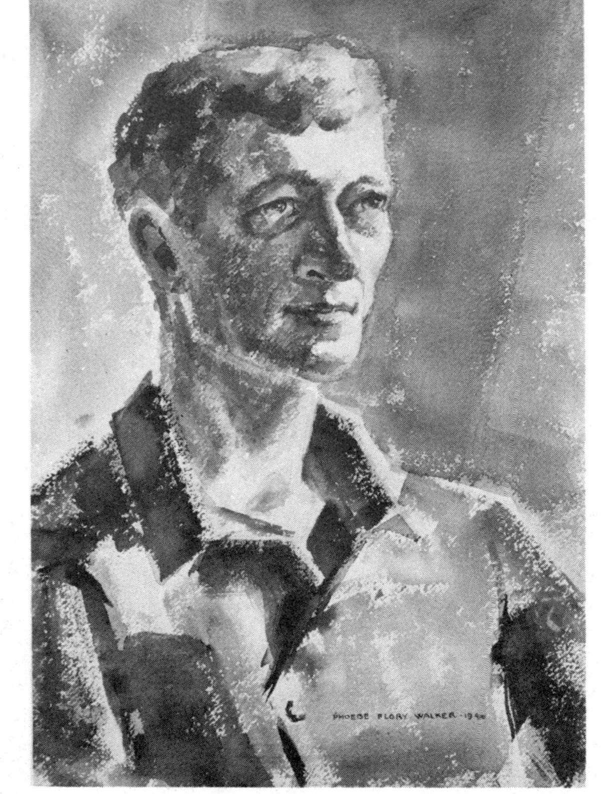

PLATE 40. Phoebe Flory: "Malcolm Ross." The final rough-brushed strokes permit the cool preliminary painting to show through.

effort. If the artist is at ease in his medium, he can keep himself receptive to all subtle impressions, and the characterization clarifies as he works. In all portraiture, however, it is desirable to formulate at least the general intention at the start and to let it be a guide throughout the painting. This habit is particularly important when working on the rapidly drying smooth paper.

P.F.

CHAPTER XIX

THE HANDLING OF SMOOTH PAPER

SINCE we first recommended rough paper, it is presumed that all your portraits so far have been on that type of surface. By now, with your increased skill with the brush and the accelerated pace gained through quickies and wet blending, it might be well to enlarge your field of direct painting by exploring the technical limitations and advantages of smooth paper.

If the two types of surfaces were greatly enlarged, a cross section would reveal hills and valleys in the rough paper. The fact that these valleys can hold considerable water and that the fiber is looser (because the handmade papers have not been pressed or rolled) accounts for the prolonged drying time of rough paper. When smooth paper is initially dampened for a wash, less water is required, and because the excess slides off so readily, the paper dries almost immediately. The artist, consequently, must work with greater speed or tackle smaller areas.

Balancing this technical limitation of smooth paper are its compensating advantages of clear color and definitive textures.

Reverting to the cross section of the rough paper, we see that each projection in the surface casts a shadow, giving an over-all gray effect. If you place samples of each type side by side, you will notice how much whiter the smooth one appears. Pigments on rough paper, of course, will likewise be neutralized, just as if gray paint had been added to the wash; in values, the darks are diminished by being interspersed with the highlighted bumps. On smooth paper, therefore, the watercolorist may achieve not only the clearest and most subtle color, but also the richest darks and the most gleaming whites.

Although, except for very fast or very dry strokes, he is limited in the use of rough brushing, he will find compensating textural effects, as did Charles Demuth in "Dancing Sailors" (Plate 37). Sharp edges can be sharper, a fluid line more controlled. The fine lines of the whisking stroke remain delicately defined. Because there are no protective valleys for paint to lodge in, pigment can be more readily removed, making for clearer wipe-outs, knife strokes, and oozles. Because of the rapid drying, paint does not flow away so easily and, by tipping the board, it may be guided into the desired area and allowed to dry before it has a chance to flow back into the wash. This device has been used to advantage both for purposes of design and of modeling by George Biddle in "Emporium" (Plate 38). A much greater concentration of moisture in one part of a tinted area will cause paint to dry at the edge of the puddle with a hard line. This effect can serve to break up the monotony of a smooth wash with tiny veins of color, as may be noted, especially of the background areas, in "Emporium."

Since a hard-surfaced smooth paper does not absorb much water, drying takes place from the surface. A diluted wash, therefore, dries more rapidly than a thick, viscous application of paint.

Because the timing and textures differ so radically between the two types of paper, it is suggested that before you embark on a smooth-paper portrait you take time out to become acquainted with the surface. Give yourself a "brush drill," making the samples suggested in Chapter X, "Surface Textures," and inventing as many new ones as you can devise. Return to Chapter VI, "Modeling with Paint," and master each of the abstract exercises before you attempt a portrait.

We have already mentioned that, in applying a graded wash to smooth paper, less water will be needed to dampen the surface; it must also be evenly distributed with more speed. One accomplishes this by tipping the smooth paper more than one would the rough. This compels the use of less water to achieve an equal darkness of value. When pigment is applied there is less time to modify it.

Where Chapter VI has suggested varying the transitions from light to shadow with rough brushing, you may now make transitions by whisking. Remember, however, that since the fine lines are so clearly defined on smooth paper, they must be executed with the greatest delicacy.

Because it is easier to remove pigment from smooth paper, you will have to use the greatest caution in wiping out a reflected light, lest it emerge as light in value as the directly illuminated portions.

The greatest difficulty will probably be encountered in splicing, again because paint is so easily removed. After the first area has been painted, tapered off, and allowed to dry, start the second. Paint up to the junction, being careful not to double paint it; quickly rinse the brush and, with a lighter value, overlap the tapered edge of the first section, blending it off with a single stroke. To stroke a second time would only remove both layers of paint.

After you have become accustomed to the pace required by smooth paper and explored its textural possibilities, try a portrait in black and white. You may find that the sections you used in the black and white portrait on rough paper are too large for you to complete easily before the drying sets in. Why not, therefore, divide the head into more and smaller sections? This will give you plenty of practice in splicing and in matching values. Compensating, however, for these early difficulties, this first portrait on smooth paper will immediately delight you with the greatly expanded range of values, and will, we hope, lead you on to try your hand at color.

When you come to color, you will find that by adhering to the staining palette, you will have fewer of the difficulties due to picking up a previously dry paint, although, on the other hand, the thin dye colors dry more quickly than the body colors.

Since the smooth-paper technique is almost like another medium, it is advisable not to keep switching back and forth between the two papers. Constant readjustments of painting habits are apt to be confusing and frustrating. If you are interested, therefore, in expanding your portrait vocabulary to include smooth paper, it would be wise to go back and retrace this series of experiments in the various methods, applying them to the new paper. The effects, of course, will be entirely different. Figure and portrait quickies, for example, while not interspersed much with rough brushing (caused often more by speed than by intention), will have even more sparkle in color. In the wet-blended and white-paper portraits, likewise, the values and colors will have greater range both in brilliance and in subtlety.

This chapter concludes our discussion of the various methods of painting watercolor portraits directly, that is, of achieving the desired color and value in the first drying time. The resulting freshness is one of watercolor's chief charms, but the medium is by no means limited to direct painting. A solidly constructed picture—one built up by layers of paint overlaid—is as possible in watercolor as in oil, tempera, pastel, or gouache, and can offer effects as rich and as glowing. The following chapters describe two such methods, whereby one may organize a portrait gradually, while still maintaining and sometimes even enhancing its color vibrancy.

P.F.

CHAPTER XX

UNDERPAINTING ON ROUGH AND SMOOTH PAPERS

When colors are mixed by the eye they give a richer, more vibrant effect than when they are mixed on the palette. This is the principle underlying broken color. A fine line of red next to a fine line of blue results in a hue that appears more intense than any ready-made violet. Broken color is two-dimensional mixing, but colors can also be mixed in depth, and that is the theory behind underpainting. By painting an area first in one color and then overlaying it with a contrasting one, a similar, although more subtle, process of color blending takes place.

It is obvious, therefore, that to be effective the two layers of paint must contrast. If they fail to, the area, compared to the rest of the picture, goes dead. Five factors are to be considered:

1. Value. The underpainting must always be lighter than the finished picture.

2. Hue. You may use either a warm or a cool underpainting, but it should never be exactly the same as the overpainting.

3. Intensity. If the first layer is slightly neutralized, the second may be executed in more intense hues. Likewise, an area that will eventually be gray is much enlivened by an intense underpainting.

4. Texture. A simple, rather smooth underpainting

will permit the maximum range of textures in the overpainting.

5. To maintain these contrasts, the two layers should not flow together.

It is evident from the foregoing that the underpainting should never dominate the finished picture. It serves merely to enhance it.

These five principles may be used by those who underpaint in any medium. Now let us see what they mean to the watercolor portraitist.

Although the drawing may be done in pencil, it is probably better to draw with the brush. Either a fine, long-haired brush, such as the rigger, or a large pointed brush will hold enough paint to sustain a long, free-flowing line. The color should be different from that which you intend to use in the underpainting. The composition, placement of the figure, characteristic shape of the head, and location of the principal features are all that is necessary. Further definition will be carried out in the under- and overpainting.

1. Value. The watercolorist reserves white paper for his lights, just as some tempera painters reserve for this purpose the gleaming white gesso. The watercolor painter may then apply very light, diluted washes over the areas to be medium and dark. Very diluted, since he will deepen the values with the overpainting. This enables him to arrange his light and dark pattern and to model the figure. Minor corrections may be made in the drawing and the likeness established. In the underpainting for "Malcolm Ross" (Plate 39), the shadow down the front of the face, the ear, and parts of the shirt were the only dark values. The rest of the painting represented the middle value, with the white paper serving for the lightest.

2. Hue. A cool underpainting will, of course, contrast with flesh tones. If you underpaint in a warm color, select one that is not identical with your subject's complexion. If, for example, his tends toward the oranges, you could use a neutral red or yellow, or even violet.

3. Intensity. Since the staining watercolors are apt to be extremely intense, care should be taken not to use them in their full strength. If you do, you will run the danger of having the underpainting dominate the picture. The exception, of course, is when treating very neutral areas. In that case, a brown may be greatly enlivened by an intense orange or red showing through, or a gray by the hint of a bright cool color beneath. When any two staining colors are mixed they will be sufficiently neutralized: alizarin and thalo blue; thalo green and orange (which may approach the color of "terre verte"); alizarin and thalo green in the same proportions make gray, or the mixture may be flavored more with one or the other; or any other combination may be used.

4. Texture. The underpainting is often best executed in solid washes, as a foil for rough brushing or whisking textures to go on top. It is a matter of choice whether the underpainting has sharp edges, as in the portrait of Malcolm Ross, or the soft edges attained by wet blending. If the latter is used, great care must be taken to keep the paint from flowing into the light areas.

5. To isolate the two layers of paint, as in any medium, the underpainting must be thoroughly dry before one proceeds. In watercolor, this means that not only must the paint be set, but the paper itself bone dry, a point especially to be borne in mind if the sheet has been thoroughly saturated for a wet-blended underpainting. Since both layers of paint are soluble in the same medium and

since the pigment paints are easily removed, as was explained in Chapter IV, "A Staining and Transparent Palette," it is recommended that you use only the staining colors. They will soak into the paper and remain relatively undisturbed by subsequent overpainting. For added insurance that the two layers will remain separated, you may cover the underpainting with a coat of clear acrylic. If no acrylic colors are used, the picture may still be classified as "transparent watercolor."

Having established the design and dispensed with the problems of structure and likeness in the underpainting, the artist is now free to develop his color pattern, augment the values, and enrich the textures.

To avoid an unpleasant iridescent effect, there should be a play between the transparent and the more opaque areas. In general, shadows are more transparent, and highlights (because light is reflected away from the surface and not absorbed) appear more opaque. This variety may be achieved by the selection of paints and the manner in which they are applied.

The watercolorist may overpaint some passages with the more opaque pigment paints and others with the transparent dyes. If he wishes thus to vary his colors, he should have at hand two palettes, one for each type, and both arranged in a corresponding order so that similar hues will be in similar locations on both palettes.

He may also vary the transparency by textures. Solid washes are more opaque. Broken color allows more of the underpainting to show through. It is in this respect that there occurs the principal difference in the handling of an underpainted portrait on rough paper and one on smooth paper. On the former, the texture may be broken by rough brushing (Plate 40), on the latter by the divided-hair or whisking stroke (Plates 41 and 42).

When using rough paper, you would do well to read again Chapter XIII on "The Rough-brushed Method." You will need the same materials: flat brushes, varying in widths; rough paper, sponged and dried; and another piece of rough paper, on which to sample brush strokes. The sample sheet should be divided into parts that are painted with the same values as in your underpainting. This will enable you to test your strokes against the backgrounds on which they will appear in the picture. As soon as you test a stroke on this sheet, it will be evident that if your underpainting is of a cool color, it will neutralize the flesh tones. You may, therefore, hit the intensity of the overpainting harder than in a directly painted portrait. Conversely, since a warm underpainting would reinforce the warmth of flesh tones, the overpainting color in that case would have to be more neutral. The values are likewise affected, and may be tested on the sample sheet against the corresponding value of the underpainting.

As in the directly painted rough-brushed portrait, it will add interest to your picture if you vary the width of the strokes and the degree of rough or solid textures, and again, aim to get the proper value and color in one shot. In most cases, the hues will have to be mixed on the palette. The effect of broken color is achieved only when the brush strokes are fine, a technique which is best adapted to smooth paper.

A portrait underpainted on smooth paper can attain a greater richness of color than can any other technique of watercolor, and this because of three factors: the smoothness of the surface, the blending of color in depth, and the use of broken color.

The overpainting must always be applied with as little pressure of the brush and as little moisture as possible.

To flood a section or to attempt to mix colors on the paper will only damage the layer beneath, even though it was executed with staining paints. Care must be taken not to stroke a second time over a damp area. Since smooth paper dries so rapidly, however, you will not have long to wait before you can reinforce it.

In the passages where you wish the underpainting to show through, you may use the transparent palette, and may also use the broken textures of the divided-hair or whisking stroke.

If a large part of the overpainting is to be executed with the whisking stroke, you may build up the composition one color at a time. It would be well to start with the hue that is most important in your color design, applying it heavily where it predominates, and whisking lightly where you wish merely to echo it in another part of the painting or to use it to modify a future color.

As soon as that is dry, you may load your brush with another color and, just as the tempera painter may build up his tones by crosshatched lines, you may cross the direction of your previous ones, although preferably not at right angles. The directions of the strokes used in the illustration, "Sam," are more evident in the detail reproduced with it (Plate 42).

It is possible to build up a painting with layers of blue, green, yellow, red, and so forth, but remember that too many transparent passages consisting of too many colors tend to give an unpleasant iridescent effect.

Underpainting enables the artist to build up the entire composition in several stages, instead of completely finishing one area at a time. Since the drying time is a negligible factor in these methods, there is little adjustment in pace

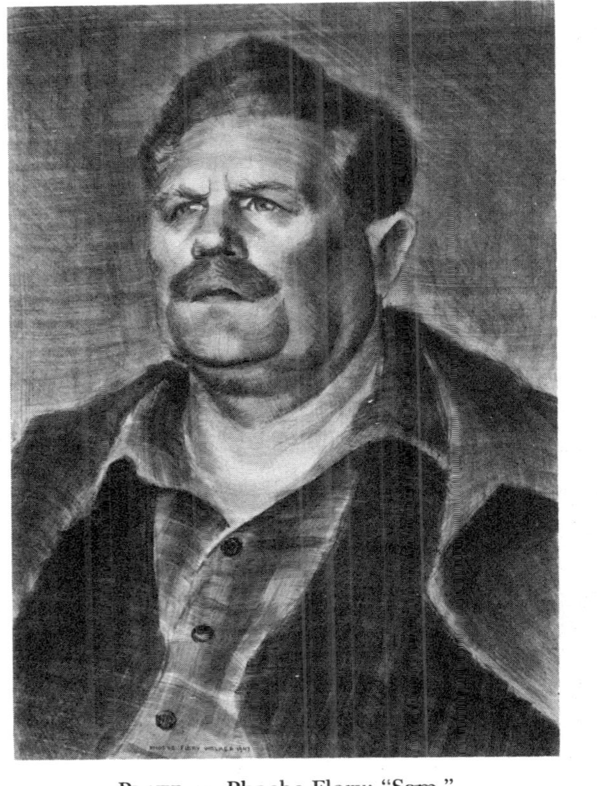

PLATE 41. Phoebe Flory: "Sam."

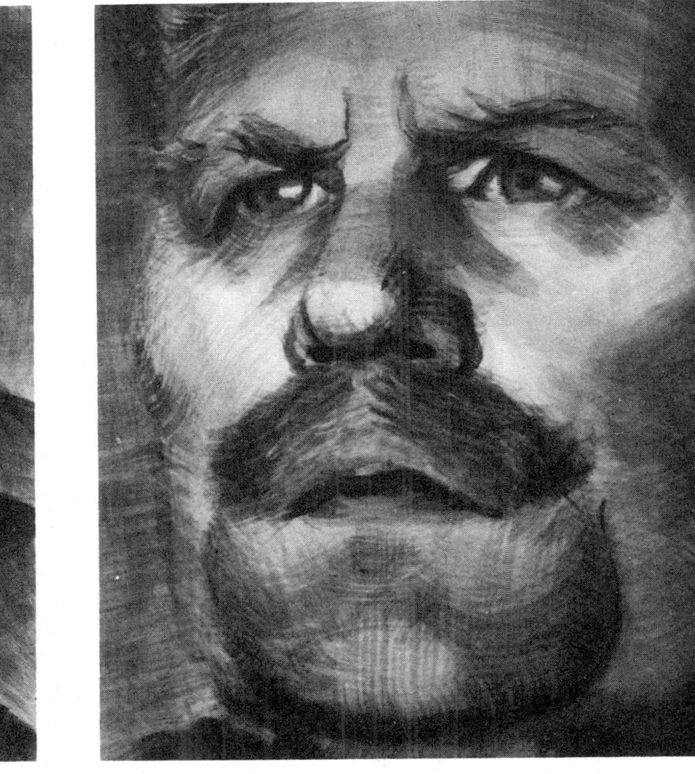

PLATE 42. Phoebe Flory: "Sam"—detail.

The smooth washes of the underpainting contrast with the broken texture of the crosshatched whisking strokes.

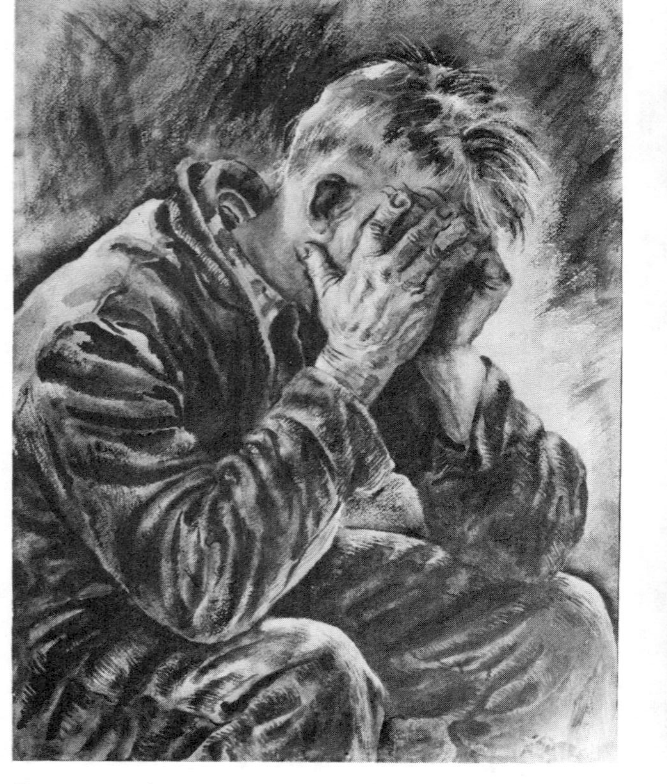

PLATE 43. Greta Matson: "Grief." Single washes combined with reinforced areas in mixed technique.

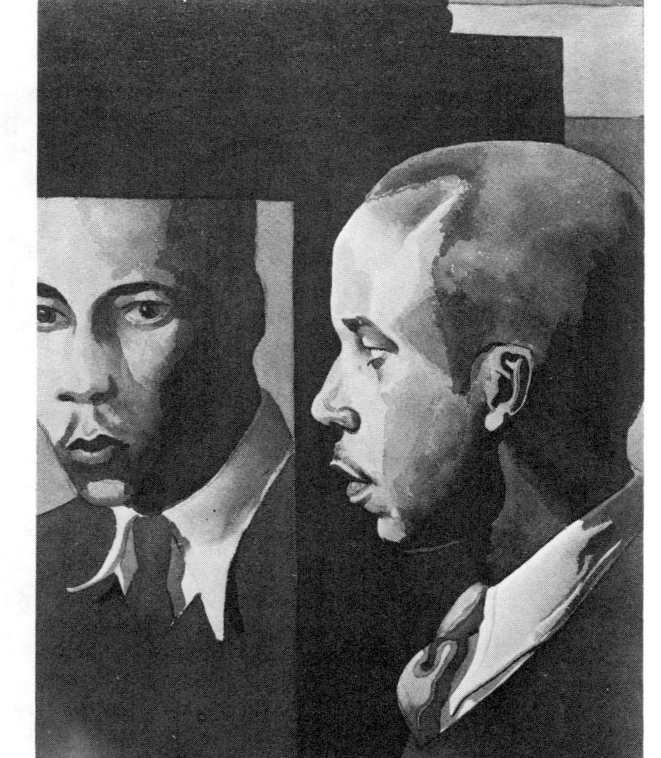

PLATE 44. Samuel Joseph Brown: "Self-Portrait." Bold, sure portraiture, effected through mixed technique. *Courtesy of the Metropolitan Museum of Art.*

from that of oil painting. Because you are not hurried, however, does not mean you should allow the picture to become labored and overdetailed. If you do, you will lose the textural interest and vibrant color.

Should you not wish to underpaint in a monochrome, the mixed technique, described in the next chapter, results in quite different effects.

P.F.

CHAPTER XXI

MIXED TECHNIQUE

ANOTHER popular variation of the watercolor medium is one we call "mixed technique." Its flexibility, due to the full range of brush treatments possible, imposes comparatively few restrictions on the painter. Like underpainting, it involves the use of superimposed washes, achieves its effect through the contrast and interplay among the various layers of paint, and accomplishes most of the modeling in the first wash.

In Chapter XX we discussed the method of underpainting in a color contrasting with subsequent washes. While the first wash in underpainting is a monochrome, the original layer of mixed technique may be in full color. Color contrast is not so essential in this technique, chiefly because the overpainting need not cover the entire area. If the artist so desires, the original wash may stand as the final one in some portions, and only isolated areas be reinforced. Since the modeling of the volumes is done at the start, the successive washes may, if the painter wishes, serve merely to darken and emphasize or enrich significant areas. As in underpainting, the preliminary wash should be lighter in value than the later ones, and the painter must plan for this in advance. If, however, certain areas should dry lighter than he anticipates, the artist may correct this condition by carefully working over that part.

The effect of reinforced washes is appropriate in the

portrayal of certain types of subjects. Some painters prefer this treatment for less delicate subjects—particularly men —and feel that it interprets the more rugged kinds of character better than the spontaneous and direct approach.

It may be used as a complete process, or, when necessary, as a remedy for errors made in the direct approaches. If skillfully handled, supplementary washes can produce almost the same effect as a single wash. You may note in the frontispiece, "Toni in Yellow," and also in "Armed Guard" (Plate 19), that most of the passages have been overpainted, though the edges are carefully blended in some portions to disguise that fact.

Through experience the painter will learn to judge accurately the amount of water required. Freshness depends on one's skill in blending smooth edges and combining pigments.

There are certain limitations and difficulties that it is well to bear in mind. One of the chief dangers is "indeterminate" color. This is sometimes referred to as "muddy" color, and results usually from the painter's inability to make up his mind. In an original wash he may experiment with color from one end of the spectrum to the other, so long as the paper remains wet, and so long as it emerges ultimately with a definite hue and saturation. But, when working over an already dry area, there can be no "muddling." The tone must be put down accurately at once when the superimposed layer is rough brushing or a smooth wash, because, except with staining colors, the original paint will be disturbed by the friction of the brush. Because of this, staining colors may best be used for the preliminary washes. For the same reason, wipe-outs during the second wash are exceedingly difficult.

The most important rule in this method demands that each layer must be completely dry before the successive one is applied. Failure to heed this results in a condition impossible to remedy. Greta Matson and Samuel Joseph Brown, in Plates 43 and 44, both show mastery of the intricacies of this technique, as do B. Fleetwood-Walker and Jacques Thevenet in their subtle characterizations (Plates 45 and 46).

Overpainting may be done in smooth washes or in any of the variations of rough brushing and whisking. If it is a large section, it may be painted solid and rough brushed at the edges to fuse it with the first wash. Or the entire area may be smoothly washed and blended at the edges as in the frontispiece, "Toni in Yellow." This can be done by first lightly dampening it, so as not to disturb the first coat of paint, and then introducing the color, or by applying the color in the center of the space, then spreading it and "finishing" the edges with a brush from which most of the water has been squeezed. A puddle caused by too much water leaves a hard rim.

Where a shadow is dark as it turns into the light—as on the shaded side of the nose when light falls from the opposite side—the reinforcing layer may be rough brushed next to the highlight and blended on the other edge as it turns into the cheek, where the gradation is less abrupt.

Should a large continuous area—such as the shadow from the hairline to the chin—be reinforced, the entire portion should be dampened and treated within one drying period, in order to avoid a patched look caused by seams.

If the portrait is being carried out in a more or less dry style, the entire portion of an area may be rough brushed. Remember that the overlapping of rough-brushed or

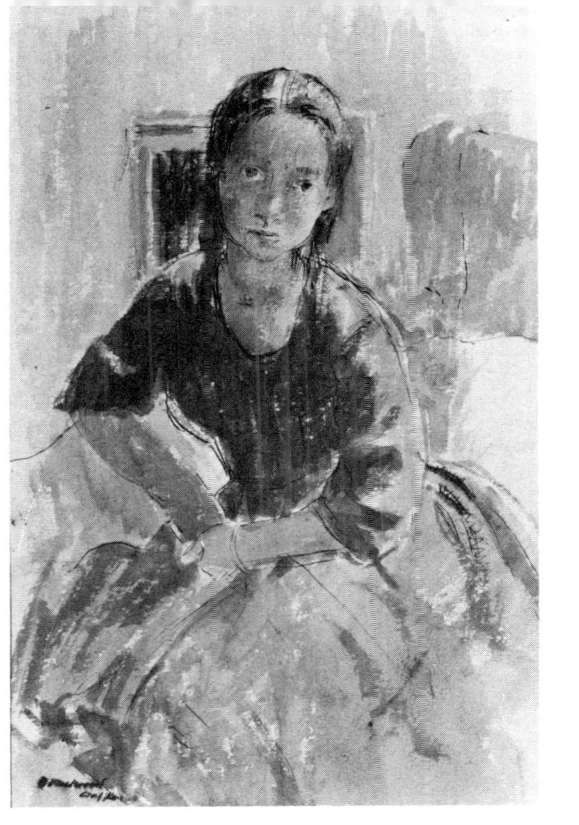

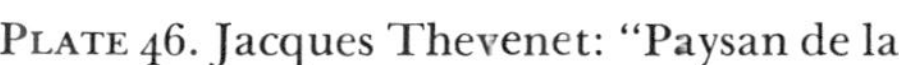

watercolor on toned paper).

Plate 46. Jacques Thevenet: "Paysan de la Nièvre."

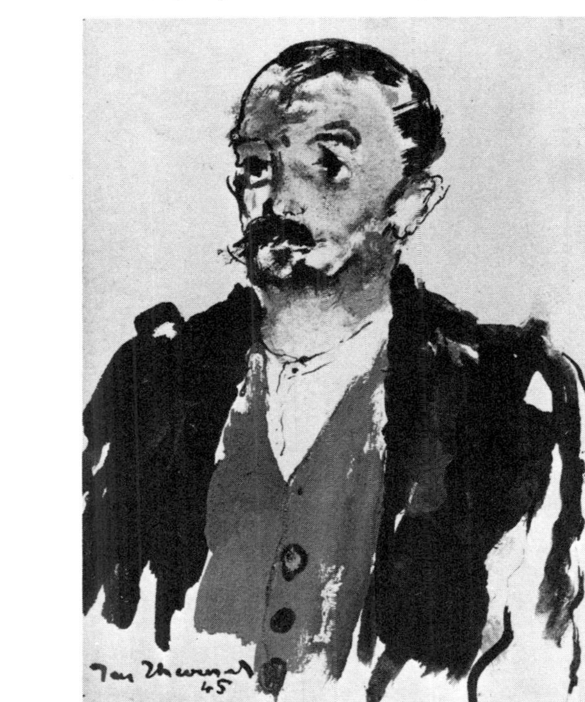

An English and a French painter interpret through similar mixed mediums two divergent personalities.

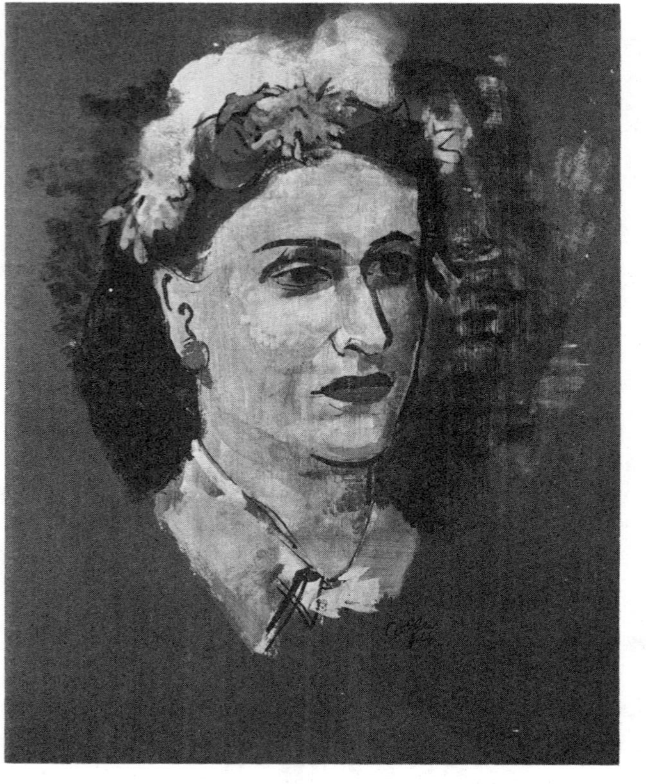

PLATE 47. William H. Calfee: "Portrait of Mrs. Theodore Eliot" (gouache). Form was developed through areas of color, line added later as accent or decoration.

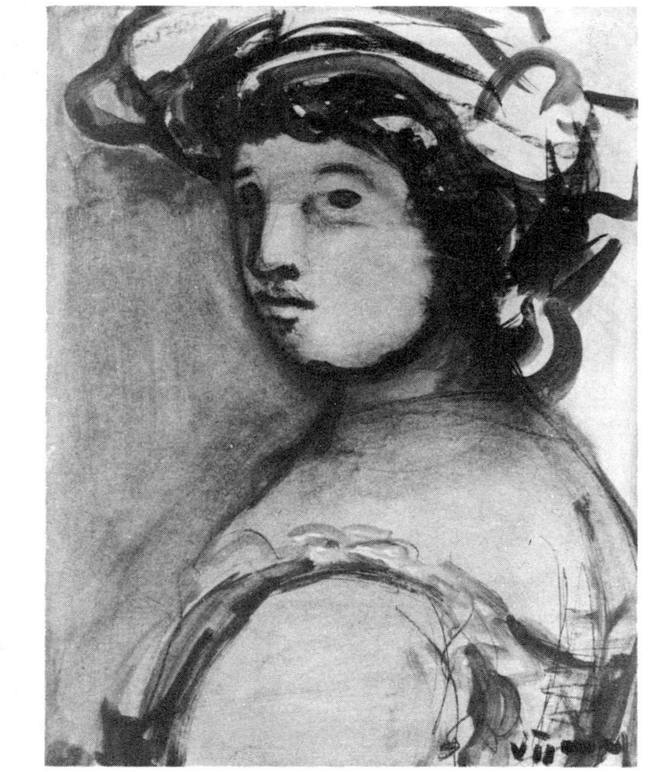

PLATE 48. Sylvain Vigny: "Buste de Femme" (gouache). Brush strokes may be broad and still sensitive and vigorous. *Courtesy, M. Caumont, Paris*

whisking strokes tends to make an area solid because it is double-painted. You may prevent the striped evidence of strokes by scumbling or blending the still damp edges, to join them.

Since the principal reason for using watercolor is to achieve a fresh, un-worked-over look, a painting that requires too many or too drastic changes is best discarded in favor of a new start. Often, however, a small portion of the wrong color, value, or texture causes a discord in the entire composition, and can easily be remedied. If cleverly done, no one need be the wiser. Whole areas may be removed, if necessary, and repainted. Seldom is it possible to lighten successfully an area in this way, but the color may be changed or darkened, and remain almost as fresh as the original wash. To do this, flood the area, then gently sponge or stroke till the desired effect is obtained, and repaint. By holding the picture under the faucet and washing the entire surface, taking care not to scrub too hard, you can side-step the problem of edges, but, at the same time, will sacrifice forever the sparkling effect of pure white highlights, and dull the crispness of rough-brushed passages. In certain types of painting, of course, this is an advantage.

Where a sharp, light accent is desired, you may use the eraser. Dampen the area with a brush, let the moisture set a moment, blot and wait about ten seconds for it to dry, then gently stroke with the eraser until the desired lightness is attained. If done too vigorously, this will remove or roughen the paper. It is best to do it gently and risk having to repeat the process. Another means of getting a sharp-edged light is actually to cut away a piece of the paper with a razor blade or stencil knife. Cut around the portion, then scrape till the white of the paper shows through.

The mixed technique, when used as a method, should be planned carefully in advance and kept as fresh as possible. As a remedy, it should serve only as a last resort. Guard against reliance upon it, for through its constant use, there is the danger of repetition and monotony in all your paintings.

D.S.

CHAPTER XXII

GOUACHE OR OPAQUE WATERCOLOR

WATER-MIXED paints may be subdivided into such mediums as egg tempera, poster paint, cement and plaster mixtures, casein paint, transparent watercolor, sumi, colored inks, and gouache. The last earns its name "opaque watercolor" through the addition of white or other opaque pigment to one's colors.

Mechanically, the two chief differences between gouache and transparent watercolor lie in the fact that with the former, one may repaint as in oil, and that one may use a board or canvas, instead of paper, on which to work.

In spite of "specifications" on printed invitations to enter pictures in exhibitions, there is a certain laxity in admitting different mediums to showings of so-called "watercolors" and "paintings." Among the latter ("painting" usually means oil) there may sometimes be found a few in egg tempera or in gouache. Burchfield seems to be one of the few watercolorists whom constituted authorities fail to recognize as submitting a painting in gouache or some other medium. This interchanging of mediums does not detract a jot from my admiration for Charles Burchfield, nor for the talent of Leon Kroll, whose inclusion in watercolor exhibits proves that the reverse situation is also sometimes true. On congratulating him once on a picture in a Chicago International Watercolor

Exhibition, I was surprised to have him say:

"Why, I have never painted a watercolor; that picture was an oil on paper that a dealer sent in."

Incidentally, you also might try oils on paper, a very flexible technique, especially in the hands of such skilled craftsmen as Mr. Kroll, or Edna Hibel of Boston.

Other examples of mixed mediums are drawings in ink, pencil, or charcoal, illuminated with light washes of watercolor or colored inks. One finds watercolors sometimes combined with a little pastel to correct—secretly—a bad spot in a wash, nip out a highlight, or cover a mistake. There are also transparent watercolors, where certain areas of gouache in a lighter value cover dark passages and thus solve the inherent difficulty of having one color show through another.

Let us try not to think of gouache, however, merely as an easy remedy. Not only are there probably as many modes of gouache painting as there are of oil, but the former, in spite of its being aqueous in nature, is closely allied to oil. In fact, almost anything that you can do with oils (except paint in the rain) you can effect as well with gouache.

For this medium one uses a stiff board with a paper or gesso surface, a canvas board, illustration board, or any heavy watercolor paper, although if thick paint is used paper will buckle. This should be placed on an easel, or held at right angles to the painter's line of sight, to avoid distortion. The surface may be white or tinted.

For a palette, a piece of window glass on a table beside you is best. Under it put a sheet of paper slightly darker than that upon which you are to work, but of the same hue, so that your mixtures of colors will look right. Gouache, like watercolor, will be lighter after it is dry than while you are working with it. This use of a palette darker than your paint is one of those minor self-deceptions, like the habit of setting watches a few minutes ahead so that one may be on time for appointments.

Brushes are soft flat bristles from one-quarter inch to one inch wide, and a few sables, both pointed and flat. An extra jar of water is needed in which to stand the brushes when they are not in use. Since gouache dries more quickly than oil and very hard, brushes need special care.

As you will, in the end, evolve a series of colors that suits you, try any that curiosity or the vagaries of other students or teachers suggest. One of these sets of pigments could be the following tubes of watercolor:

Light red, burnt sienna, burnt umber, yellow ocher, strontian yellow, viridian, cobalt blue, ivory black, and white. These are all oxides. In thick mixtures of paint like oils or gouache, when these oxide colors are used with sulphide colors such as cadmiums or ultramarine or vermilion, they are not always chemically inert and permanent. [Most colors nowadays mix more safely than when Eliot O'Hara wrote this chapter. P.F.] Gouache means opaque watercolor, whether the paints are bought mixed, or are compounded by the artist. The combination of any transparent color with any opaque one is never transparent.

Decide whether you intend to paint a picture that will have the whole surface covered, or whether it will be the kind of painting in which the colors are sketched onto a background that shows through here and there, or allows the elements to be vignetted.

In either case the mechanics are the same, although the method of working may further branch off into almost any sort of mannerism or personal quality known to either oil painting or watercolor.

Gouache thus becomes a most elastic medium and one with which either the oil painter or the watercolorist may quickly feel at home.

Before starting a gouache, as with any other kind of picture, it is well to experiment with mixtures of paint. The person accustomed to watercolor may at first produce a chalky white quality, from using too much white in mixtures. Indeed, this cold gray flesh tone is also a frequent initial mistake with oil students who may have been left too much to their own devices. A large crop of such El Greco-like color schemes without El Greco's other qualities is the product of a school where color mixing has not been emphasized.

Mixtures should not, in other words, contain too much white and black paint, but be composed of the various colors themselves. Do not consider paint mixtures as if they were either all white tinted with watercolor or all color darkened with black.

It is best to squeeze out on the palette only a small amount of each pigment needed, as these colors dry very quickly, so quickly that a palette knife is hardly necessary for mixing. A painting knife, however, or other small pointed tool, is often useful in obtaining various surface textures or in laying on a highlight.

Many painters in gouache, instead of starting with a palette all set up with colors, squeeze them out of the tube at the time of using them almost as if they were going directly onto the brush or paper.

In matching or coining a color start with a small squeeze of the most suitable one, and modify that first with other colors. Add merely the minimum of black or white required, and then only after it is found that the yellow will not make it light enough or the umber dark enough.

In blending one hue into another there are several procedures. One is to paint half the area with the one color and the other half with the other; then, while they are both wet, to take a brush containing a mixture of both and to start in the center stroking both ways. Another method is to drag one over another with the brush or finger. If one of the colors has become dry, a stroke of the other, lightly laid on, will remain pure, although the underneath color, if rubbed with a bristle brush, can be loosened and will mix with the new one.

In cases where a blending is desired but there is danger of interfering with adjacent satisfactory passages, try using a pointed sable brush. Charge it with paint and then pinch it between the thumb and finger until it is a chisel shape or resembles a flat brush, and the top edge or point has now become a series of single hairs or small brushes. Dip them carefully on the palette and, by whisking lightly over a darker or lighter area, you may apply a fine series of shading lines which can be superimposed or crossed or even blurred later with the finger.

Your initial testing of the possibilities of gouache should take the form of producing sample patches of a graded set of values from white to black, and of each color from lightest to darkest in its most saturated or brilliant state.

This should be followed by a series of stripes of each color shown in one value but blending from the most brilliant to gray. Since, in realistic painting, flesh color is usually warm, pay particular attention to the oranges and reds.

In all of this experimenting you will be learning to allow for the difference in value between wet and dry paint, and will be able to gauge the graying and lightening action, particularly of the middle and dark values, as they dry.

If you have trouble in determining the amount of allowance to make, try duplicating those first sample patches and stripes after they are dry, as was recommended for the samples in the wet-blending chapter. In this way you will be matching a wet color against a dry one.

It is a good practice, for large areas, to mix a quantity of the desired colors (as much as can be kept wet) and try them out briefly for value before going ahead with the modeling.

Many painters block in a face with two tones—light side and dark side—making them warmer and darker than ultimately desired, and then paint over and into them with the highlights and dark accents.

Another approach is the one used by William H. Calfee, in his portrait of Mrs. Eliot (Plate 47).

He contributes these paragraphs on his selection of gouache for this particular study.

A first training in sculpture has directed my painting conceptions to an interest in solid or weighty form through color. Early paintings, mostly murals, were colored drawings. Search revealed that painting meant form achieved *through* color, the opposite to no matter how well drawn a contour *filled in* with color. At one time, becoming interested in the expressive use of the brush, I did many ink and watercolor drawings trying to make the brush carry my intention. These seemed thin to me no matter how vigorous.

Gouache or tempera used opaquely has the fluidity of watercolor and at the same time a sense of solid substance. Its use on cardboard or paper allows one to do ten versions of the same design economically. This freer attitude seems to allow unworried works to *occur,* their planning having been done in preceding variations on a similar theme.

The particular painting of mine which you are using is *built up* rather than repainted. The usage "re-paint" implies "corrected" to me. If one builds to a final result, the thought process is different. As with oils or tempera, a gouache often is started with a color base which is the exact opposite of what the artist plans to be the final color, also form is developed through areas of color, line added later as accent or decoration. I realize that watercolor may be *developed* too, but the memory of the English school causes most people to think of "direct" as meaning quick, and therefore fresh.

Another suggestion which may prove useful, and I have done it in the present head, is that of starting with a "going-away-plane" color and building forward with light. This means that in the final result any area, and especially turning edges, will remain in that first-used color, which is generally of middle value and less warm, and, therefore, recedes. Deeper darks, as may be added, accent adjacent projections.

These comments help to explain Mr. Calfee's approach to opaque watercolor, and the appeal that it has for him.

"Buste de Femme" by Vigny (Plate 48) shows areas in flat washes and lines drawn with a wide brush. The difference in Vigny's technique from that of Mr. Calfee is only an indication of the wide variety of effects to which gouache invites you.

Still another watercolor medium will next be treated by a painter who is as expert in gouache as in the technique that he describes here—that of ink on scratchboard.

E.O'H.

CHAPTER XXIII

NOTES ON SCRATCHBOARD TECHNIQUE

by MITCHELL JAMIESON

ELIE FAURE has somewhere said that artists of the past, seemingly confined and restricted by having to depict scenes from the Bible or important personages of their time, were actually much more free than the modern artist. This is so because they were free to pour all they were capable of into subjects of universal significance without first having to find something new to say, then a new way of saying it. Technique and subject matter were already prescribed and taken for granted, integrated into the very thought and spirit of the time.

Certainly portraiture seems practically dead today as a form of expression for our most vital painters, compared with its life and magnificence in the past. Look at any representative show of contemporary paintings and you will be struck not only by the absence of good portraits but by the ascendancy of new and striking use of materials over content and meaning—more reliance than ever upon the expressive qualities of the medium itself, sometimes accompanied by sensitivity and restraint, sometimes not. Spiritual unrest and confusion do not create exactly the best psychological atmosphere for fine portraiture.

In the light of all this, it seems absurd to offer notes on personal technique, but I feel the prefacing remarks may be appropriate to any discussion of methods, whether or not they relate to portrait painting. Let me make it clear that: (1) I regard the medium I am to describe as supplementary to other methods of painting; (2) its use may be of greatest value in stimulating that interaction between medium and the ideas that arise partly from sensitivity to its potentialities. At its best a medium like this can be a distinct and authentic form of expression, at worst a bag of tricks something like finger painting.

The advantage of work done on scratchboard is precisely the same as that of work on a gesso ground brought to an extremely smooth finish. The surface is a polished one, absorbent and highly luminous, coated with chalk so that lights may be scraped out with the point of a sharp instrument. The basic principles involved, too, are akin to painting in tempera on a gesso ground, with the difference that inks are used instead of pigments, and applied with greater directness and speed. The scratchboard surface absorbs watercolor and tempera too readily, so I have used colored inks, working with great rapidity to obtain freshness and luminosity. (See "Child of Algiers," Plate 49.)

Inks on scratchboard have a glazelike quality and remain clear and luminous even when colored with modifying washes. I find it best to put on the pure colors as they come from the bottle (diluting as necessary, of course) in clear washes, loosely and freely, taking the utmost advantage of the brilliance of the colors against the extreme whiteness of the background. Black has an especially rich quality and can be used over other colors without destroying their life and vibrancy.

The work I have done on scratchboard has been more or less experimental and the outgrowth of a period when I felt the need to attempt greater fluency and transparency

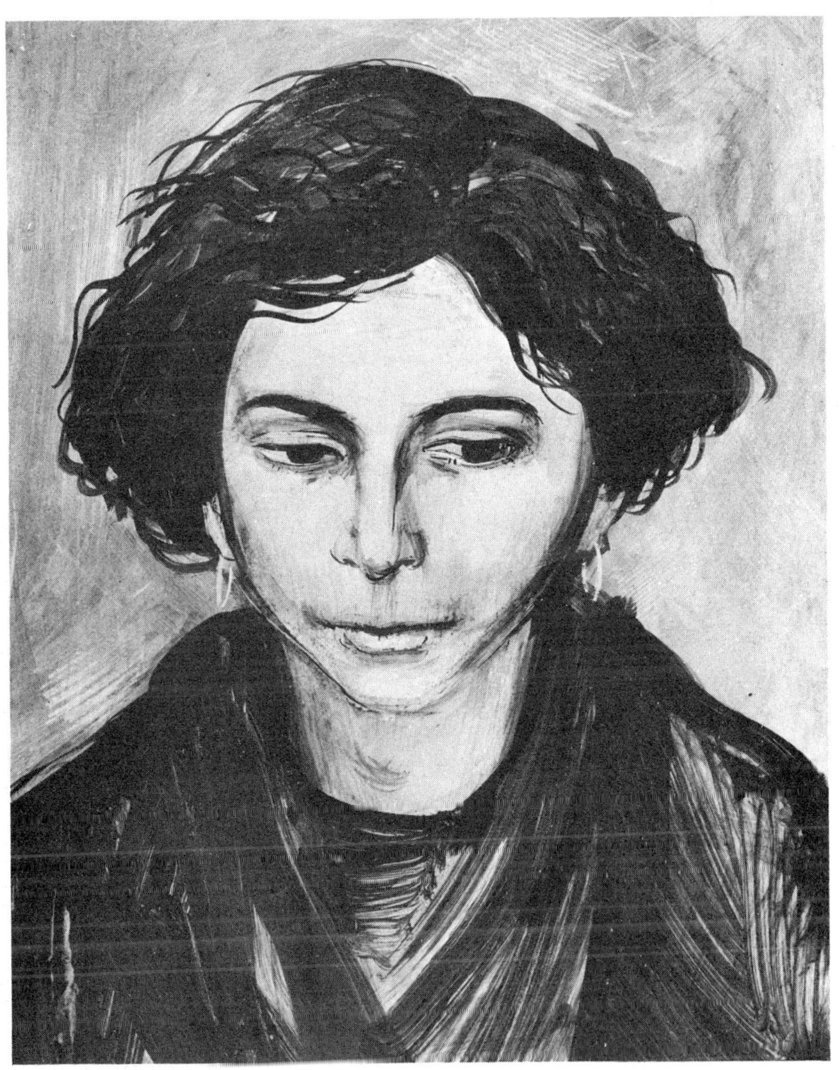

PLATE 49. Mitchell Jamieson: "Child of Algiers" (colored inks on scratchboard). Scratchboard permits incising a light line or drawing a dark one. *Courtesy, Mr. and Mrs. Paul M. Lewis, Washington, D. C.*

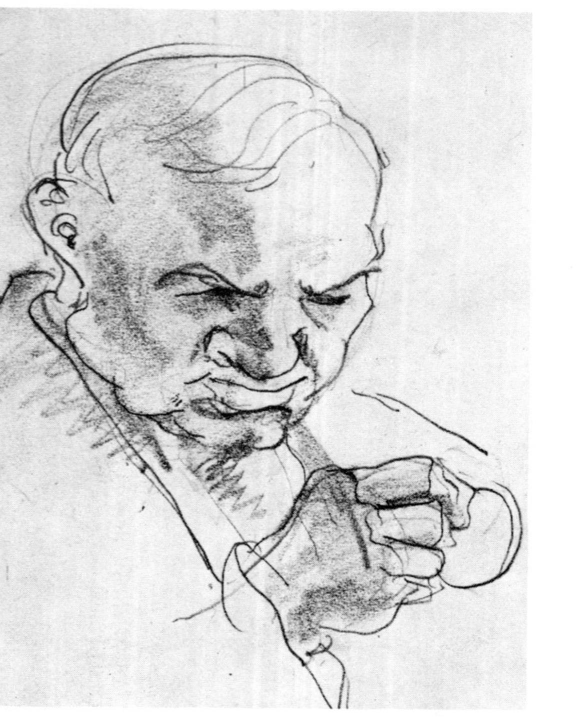

PLATE 50. Phoebe Flory: Sketch for "These Dimming Eyes" (pencil). A preliminary study for the painting, Plate 33.

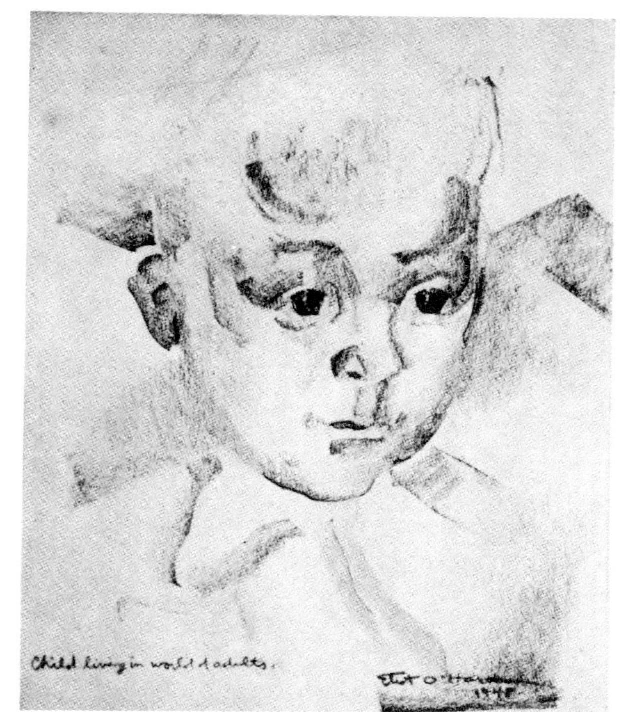

PLATE 51. Eliot O'Hara: "Child Living in a World of Adults" (graphite stick). A character study in lost and found edges.

in my painting. I have not worked in it primarily as a portrait medium nor do I claim to have developed or explored it fully. It so happens I have never seen scratchboard used before for anything but black and white work, and that mostly commercial. For all I know, however, others may have found this highly polished, brilliant surface as interesting as I have. Interesting but dangerous, for it is not at all easy to control work on such a surface, on the one hand, and on the other there are far too many opportunities for superficial cleverness of technique.

In the absence of any established method of procedure, and since painters will wish to experiment anyhow, I might simply note down one method I have used for a study of a head. Preliminary drawing was completed and traced on the painting surface in pencil, the scratchboard having first been mounted or taped firmly to some stiff backing to prevent warping or curling. Next, a very loose underpainting in brown ink, amounting to almost a mere suggestive outline. A tone of diluted yellow ink was then brushed swiftly over the entire surface of the painting to afford a warm ground of the lightest possible transparency. This yellow tone was then worked into and modified here and there with warm and cool areas. Light red, orange, and green were used. The color was brushed on rapidly and in some of the light areas of the face, scraped off with a razor blade before it had completely dried (lightly scraped, that is, leaving the yellow base tone to show through and not the white of the chalk coating).

Finally accents were added in black ink, with a pen in some places, pointed brush in others.

Another method I have used consists of covering the surface with a warm red or brown tone as a ground and scraping out the lights roughly with a razor. Local color is then applied loosely over the roughened surface, and accents added with a pen or brush. This system makes the most of the contrasts between the roughened texture of the surface where the coating has been scraped off and the smooth areas of transparent tones.

Too much scraping is to be avoided unless it can be used in a painterly way.

There are an infinite number of variations of technique that can all too easily be abused, but in the main one should be guided by the inherent qualities of freshness one finds in clear color applied to a brilliant white background, when the surface breathes through the painting layers to give it something of a life of its own.

Scratchboard comes in only one size, so far as I know, twenty-two by twenty-eight inches, and the trade name is Ross Board. Extra heavy weight is best. For permanence, it should be mounted on some stiff backing like plywood or wall board and, when framed, should be kept under glass, as the surface is as easily damaged as that of a watercolor.

Some brands of colored inks are quite opaque and somewhat like paint but on the whole I prefer the clear type. I especially like the consistency and strength of inks like turquoise, green, yellow, and black. The various colors are kept in separate cups—plastic or tin. The brush is dipped into the ink, then into water, until the proper consistency is found. The brush, loaded with color, is then tried on a piece of scrap paper before being applied to scratchboard, since it must contain exactly the right amount of color and water.

There are undoubtedly different degrees of permanence in these inks, as in pigments, but from my own observation of paintings completed within the last two years, there has been no change in intensity or brilliance.

There is no one way to use scratchboard. The similarity to a gesso surface, with its attractive characteristics, suggests many methods and approaches, all subject to free experimentation as to which allows the greatest flexibility coupled with the greatest control.

[Since publication of this book in 1949, some inks, light tested, proved to be fugitive. The serious painter, therefore, is advised to light test any inks he wishes to use. One way of testing them is as follows:

With a flat-stroke brush, paint stripes of each ink across a piece of 100 per cent rag paper. Cut another piece of paper half the width of the first paper and tape it to the painted one so that each stripe is half covered, and the other half exposed. Then tape the set, with the colors outward, in a south window. Be sure to label the name and brand of each ink and to write the date the experiment was commenced. In four to six months, remove the test and see if the segments of ink samples that were protected from the sun are the same color as those exposed to the sun. P.F.]

CHAPTER XXIV

SKETCHING AND INFORMAL PAINTING

SKETCHES not only afford good practice, but they can also be used as material for paintings. We might even say, as did Cennino Cennini, "Do not fail to draw something every day, for no matter how little it is it will be well worth while, and it will do you a world of good."

SKETCHING GEAR

Separate sheets of paper are usually better than a notebook, since they can be sorted and filed. Printers or paper dealers sell "trim" cheaply (by the pound). You often find a good grade of bond or other unglazed or even colored paper among these scraps, which you can cut into handy pocket-sized sheets.

A soft pencil gives dark lines and quickly applied shadows, while a hard pencil is sharper for delicate line work or a clean surface pattern. Carpenter's pencils or rectangular sticks of graphite are available in any degree of hardness. Use the corner for a sharp line and the broad side for a soft, wide line (which is useful to show planes or shadows in a single stroke). The sketch for "These Dimming Eyes" (Plate 50) was done with a carpenter's pencil, while "Child Living in a World of Adults" (Plate

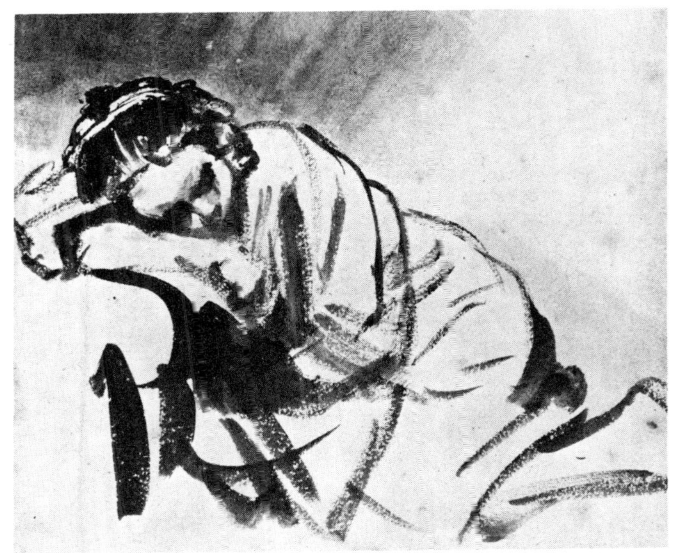

PLATE 52. Rembrandt van Ryn: "Sleeping Girl"—detail. Lines sketched with rough brushing, the face suggested by wet blending. *Courtesy, the British Museum.*

PLATE 53. Francisco de Goya y Lucientes: "Beggar Holding a Stick in His Left Hand"—detail. Incisive brush work interprets the rags as effectively as the characteristic expression of the mendicant. *Courtesy of The Metropolitan Museum of Art.*

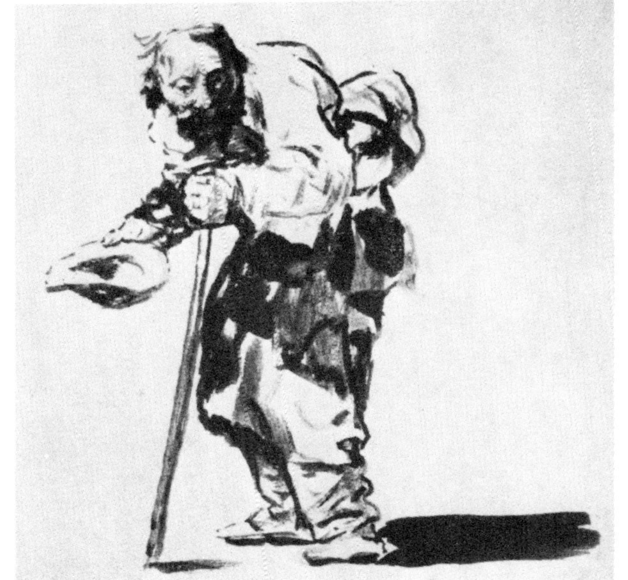

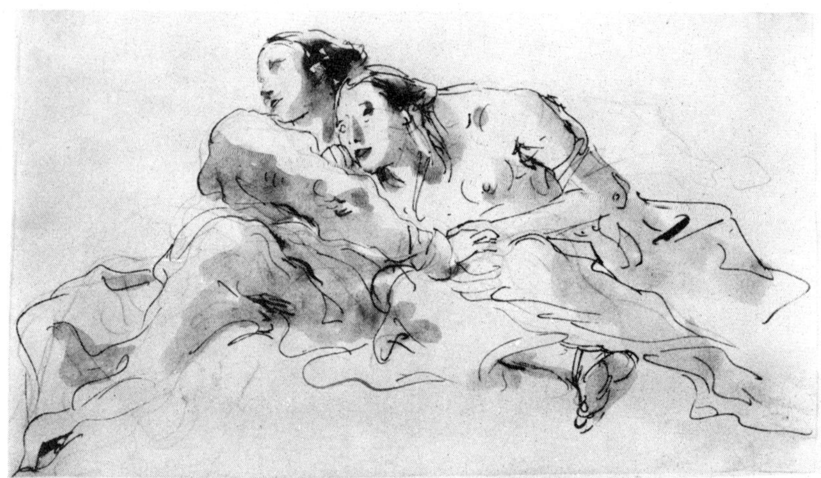

PLATE 54. Giovanni Battista Tiepolo: "Two Female Figures Seated." A fine, flowing line and undefined areas of wash suggest form as well as action. *Courtesy, The Pierpont Morgan Library.*

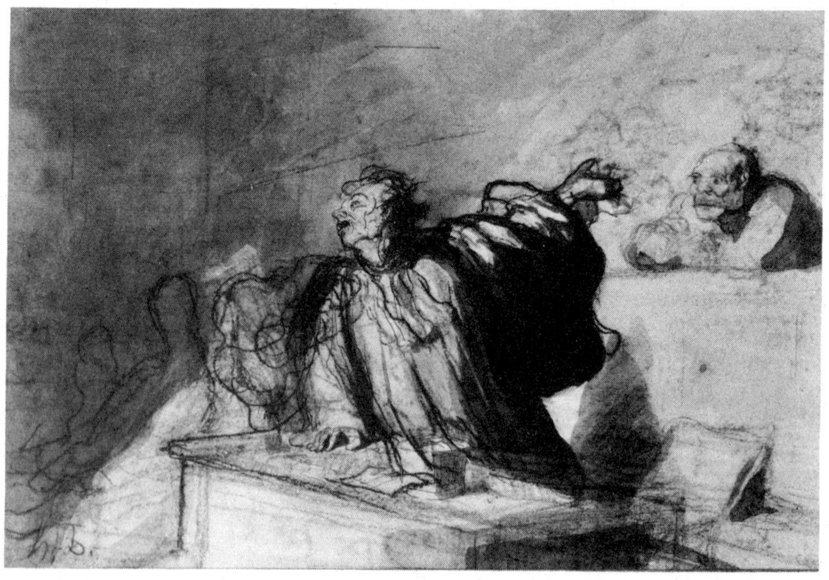

PLATE 55. Honoré Daumier: "Plea for the Defense." The rhythmic ink strokes may symbolize the rolling on of the orator's voice. *Courtesy, Phillips Gallery, Washington, D. C.*

51) was executed with varying lengths of graphite held flat.

The point of a fountain pen makes a more decisive line, or when it is turned over and the back of the nib rubbed on the paper, it deposits a larger quantity of ink. Shadows in either pen or pencil can be smeared by a moistened thumb. David Fredenthal, we are told, sketched "with one or two fountain pens, a little saliva, and rubbing with a finger."

A small piece of Negro lead, wax crayon, chalk, or conté crayon can be used endwise for a sharp line, sidewise for a broader area. If gradual pressure is exerted on one end of the flat crayon, the area will grade from dark to light. This effect can also be achieved with the felt-nibbed fountain pen equipped with interchangeable nibs. There is also a fountain brush; the pointed nylon brush is capable of both a fine line and a broad area.

Any new implement with which you sketch encourages a different technique, and changing materials from time to time gives you a refreshingly new viewpoint.

Two small wash drawings by noted painters are prized, respectively, by the British Museum and the Metropolitan: Rembrandt's "Sleeping Girl" and Goya's "Beggar Holding a Stick in His Left Hand" (Plates 52 and 53).

A mixture of mediums is also challenging, such as conté crayon with pen, or pen and wash. The latter was probably the combination used by Honoré Daumier in "Plea for the Defense" (Plate 55). For vigorous impact these sketches by both Daumier and Tiepolo (Plate 54) could rival most of the more studied studio paintings of lesser artists.

On toned paper, such as unglazed wrapping paper, one may sketch in white pencil or chalk, or combine a dark medium (ink, pencil, or crayon) with the white.

The three or four values to which one is limited in a monochrome sketch afford excellent practice in simplifying the value pattern. If the drawings are to be used as bases for future paintings, however, further notes may be recorded by a shorthand system of numbers for the values (starting with 1 for the lightest), and letters for the colors (R means red, etc.), with plus and minus signs to indicate intensity.

WHERE TO SKETCH

Quick notes may be taken on the basic form of heads or figures, facial angles, figures in action, caricatures, or facial expressions in any public place where people are working or playing: restaurants, stations, markets, busses, playgrounds, docks, or factories.

Sketches requiring more time, such as tactile drawing, or other forms of distortion, studies of planes and design, comparative analyses of hands, ages, racial types, features, etc., may best be procured where people are less active. Libraries are excellent for this sort of drawing. There, people are so interested in what they are reading that they seldom notice they are being observed, especially if you prop up a book in front of you and pretend to be taking notes. The sketch for "These Dimming Eyes" (Plate 50) was made in a library. (It may be interesting to compare it with the painting developed from it, Plate 33.)

Outdoor painting (for figure quickies, figures combined with landscape, action sketching, etc.) may be accomplished by stationing yourself wherever you won't be run over or attract too big a crowd. In congested districts you may avoid the annoyance of onlookers by painting from an automobile, although a small car necessitates a pretzel-like contortion.

INFORMAL PAINTING

We have not advocated self-portraits for the same reason that we do not advocate too much concentration on *any* one subject.

This danger in self-portraits, however, may be minimized by taking a view of yourself that you do not ordinarily see in a single mirror. By the use of two or three mirrors, you may see a three-quarter, profile, or even back view. While you are your own most patient model, that factor, in itself, may be a disadvantage. If the work becomes a struggle or you pose too long, the picture may assume a grim or even fierce expression.

Even if you do not strive for a likeness, self-portraits can be useful as experiments in a new painting technique, in lighting, design, or distortion.

You may derive excellent drawing and painting practice from volunteering to do portraits at benefit entertainments, Army, Navy, or veterans' hospitals, or other nonprofit institutions. You do not, of course, keep the results, but if you want a record, you may have them photostated and return the original to the subject. In justice, however, to the co-operation and patience of the sitter, you should not attempt this type of portrait practice until you are skilled in getting a likeness.

There are several factors that should be considered in assuming this kind of volunteer job. You learn to adjust your painting to all conditions: to paint patients or inmates who cannot be expected to hold still, or who are lying flat in bed, who are strapped into intricate contraptions, or whose faces are badly disfigured. To keep your professional and volunteer work from conflicting, adhere to a clear-cut policy concerning free or charge portraits.

After initial tries at a new technique at home or in a class, you may gain valuable additional practice by means of these volunteer portraits. They give you assurance, speed, and accuracy and a chance to develop your technique while rendering a much-needed service.

Art schools would do well to arrange regular volunteer hours in nearby hospitals for their advanced portrait students. Other institutions, such as old people's homes and orphanages, also welcome such a service, and give the painter an even broader latitude of subjects.

We cannot stress too much the importance of acquiring the habit of incessant sketching. Leonardo wrote:

> You should often amuse yourself when you take a walk for recreation, by watching and taking note of the attitudes and actions of men as they talk and dispute, or laugh or come to blows one with another—both their actions and those of the bystanders who either intervene or stand looking on at these things; noting them down with rapid strokes in this way, in a little pocket book, which you ought always to carry with you.

P.F.

CHAPTER XXV

IN CONCLUSION

WATERCOLOR portrait painters of this generation are eagerly forging ahead in varying directions. Some utilize the translucence that they feel denied in other mediums. Others reinforce this transparence with underpainting to achieve solidity and depth. Some enrich these qualities with the wealth of possible inherent textures. And still other artists combine various water-mixed paints to coin more phrases in this versatile form of expression.

We have sought to present these developments as possible springboards for new ways of interpreting people. By returning to sketching at the end of the book, we call attention to the aspect in which—perhaps above all others —watercolor is unrivaled.

Daring, speed in brush movements, the drying time of wet paper, the quickie, instantaneous decisions, and a horror of dawdling and patching up mistakes are all so much in the spirit of watercolor painting that the medium offers a challenge to press smartly ahead, to capture with speed the mutability of people. Even in paint there is some reason for the expression, "the quick and the dead."

P.F. and E.O'H.

BIOGRAPHIES

PHOEBE FLORY, Fellow of The Royal Society of the Arts (England): born in Cleveland, Ohio, 1914, daughter of painter-illustrator Julia McCune Flory. Education: A.B. Smith College (art major); Cleveland Institute of Art (portraiture major); The Art Students League, New York (with Jean Charlot); O'Hara Watercolor School. Exhibited: besides juried group exhibits, over 50 individual shows. Teaching: O'Hara Watercolor School, Cleveland Museum of Art, Cleveland Institute of Art; classes in Cleveland, Miami, Laguna Beach, New York; intensive workshops for 15 art institutes or universities; now runs The Phoebe Flory Watercolor School at 16 North Main Street, Mont Vernon, New Hampshire (accredited for graduate and undergraduate college credits), teaching watercolor portraiture. Author: (under her married name, Phoebe Flory Walker) *Portraits in the Making*, with Dorothy Short and Eliot O'Hara, G. P. Putnam's Sons, 1948; *Painting People in Watercolor* (for her students). Produced: motion picture, *Texture in Painting* (winner of the CINE Golden Eagle), shown in international film festivals at Venice, Melbourne, Adelaide, Montreal, and U.S.A.; over 50 taped slide lectures.

DOROTHY SHORT PAUL: born in Richmond, Indiana, 1920, daughter of Rear Admiral and Mrs. E. T. Short. Married Captain E. C. Paul, U.S.N. (Retired). Education: graduated from The Bishop's School, La Jolla, California; attended George Washington University; studied in China (under Paul Safonoff), 1933; Corcoran School of Art, Washington, D.C.; Cranbrook Academy of Art, Michigan; O'Hara Watercolor School. Exhibited: Washington Watercolor Club; Corcoran Gallery; San Diego Museum; Norfolk Museum of Arts and Sciences; U.S. Naval Academy; Butler Art Institute; Fine Arts Club, St. Augustine; Hoosier Show, Indianapolis; Gibbs Gallery, Charleston; Art Club of Northern Virginia; The Retired Officer's Association, Alexandria; Grand Central Galleries, New York City; Santa Barbara Art Museum; Art of the Redwoods, Gualala; Marin Arts Guild. Teaching: O'Hara Watercolor School. Co-author: *Portraits in the Making*. Now painting and teaching based at 71 San Marino Drive, San Rafael, California.

ELIOT O'HARA, N.A.: 1890–1969. Education: Massachusetts, Vermont, Paris. He managed the O'Hara Waltham Dial Company, got it out of debt. Taught himself watercolor on the weekends. Selling the factory, he provided for relatives, and devoted himself to painting full time. In 1928 he won a Guggenheim Fellowship and traveled and painted in Europe. He exhibited in Paris, London, and Soviet Armenia, the first American artist to visit Russia since 1917. In 1931 he founded the O'Hara Watercolor School, Goose Rocks Beach, Maine, where he summered for 16 years until it burned in 1947. During winters he painted, exhibited, wrote books and articles on art, taught. In 1943–44 he served on the Camouflage Section, Bureau of Ships, U.S. Navy. After the Maine fire, he traveled around the world, painting. He returned to exhibit and sell throughout the U.S.A., teaching during summers in California; Flat Rock, North Carolina; and, in 1968, Maine. He painted in Europe, Asia, Africa, North and South America, and had 235 individual shows. He is represented in 45 public collections, and won numerous awards. He wrote six books on watercolor technique; collaborated on two on portraiture. He produced over 20 art-instruction motion pictures, the majority distributed by Encyclopaedia Britannica Films, Inc.

GUEST AUTHORS

WALTER B. COLEBROOK (Chapter VI, "Modeling with Paint," Part II), 1911–1969. Art education: Norton School of Art; O'Hara Watercolor School. Teaching: Army Special Service Section; O'Hara Watercolor School, Maine; Norton School of Art; Fort Lauderdale and South Miami (often with Eliot O'Hara); Blowing Rock and Charlotte, North Carolina; Ashland, Kentucky; Muskegan and Ludington, Michigan. Poster and scenic artist; department-store display director.

MITCHELL JAMIESON (Chapter XXIII, "Notes on Scratchboard Technique"): 1915–1976. Education: Corcoran School of Art and Abbott School, Washington, D.C. Painting commissions: Treasury Department Project, Key West and Virgin Islands; *Fortune* magazine; *Life* magazine; post-office murals, Ohio and Maryland; Marian Anderson mural, Department of the Interior, Washington, D.C.; Secretary of the Treasury, Henry Morgenthau, Jr.; President and Mrs. Roosevelt, Hyde Park; recorded defense activities for Office of Emergency Management. Lieutenant, U.S. Navy, combat artist, Europe and Pacific. Awards: citation and Bronze Star Medal; two Guggenheim Fellowships for Creative Painting; grants from American Academy of Arts and Letters and National Institute of Arts and Letters. Teaching: Cornish School, Seattle; Madeira School, Virginia; Norton Gallery School of Art, Florida; Fort Worth Art Center; Corcoran School of Art, Washington, D.C. Art Commissions: N.A.S.A., Project Mercury and Saturn launching; aboard *Hornet* during lunar spacecraft recovery; Apollo 17 mission. In Vietnam, U.S. Army Office of Military History; Bureau of Reclamation, Department of Interior, in Colorado. Exhibited on West Coast and in Washington, D.C.

CARL SCHMALZ (Chapter IV, "A Staining and Transparent Palette"): born 1926. Education: A.B., Ph.D. Harvard University; O'Hara Watercolor School. Taught: O'Hara Watercolor School; Bowdoin College; currently professor of fine arts, Amherst College; conducts Carl Schmalz Watercolor Workshops, Kennebunkport, Maine; lectures, demonstrations, workshops in U.S.A. and Bermuda. Former Associate Director, Bowdoin College Museum; served on juries U.S.A. and abroad. Exhibits prints and paintings: besides group displays, over 20 individual shows; national awards; work in public and private collections. Author: *Watercolor Lessons from Eliot O'Hara*; *Watercolor Your Way*; exhibition catalogues and critiques.

A CATALOG OF SELECTED

DOVER BOOKS

IN ALL FIELDS OF INTEREST

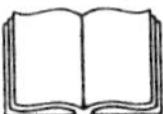

A CATALOG OF SELECTED DOVER BOOKS IN ALL FIELDS OF INTEREST

DRAWINGS OF REMBRANDT, edited by Seymour Slive. Updated Lippmann, Hofstede de Groot edition, with definitive scholarly apparatus. All portraits, biblical sketches, landscapes, nudes. Oriental figures, classical studies, together with selection of work by followers. 550 illustrations. Total of 630pp. 9⅛ × 12¼.
21485-0, 21486-9 Pa., Two-vol. set $25.00

GHOST AND HORROR STORIES OF AMBROSE BIERCE, Ambrose Bierce. 24 tales vividly imagined, strangely prophetic, and decades ahead of their time in technical skill: "The Damned Thing," "An Inhabitant of Carcosa," "The Eyes of the Panther," "Moxon's Master," and 20 more. 199pp. 5⅜ × 8½. 20767-6 Pa. $3.95

ETHICAL WRITINGS OF MAIMONIDES, Maimonides. Most significant ethical works of great medieval sage, newly translated for utmost precision, readability. Laws Concerning Character Traits, Eight Chapters, more. 192pp. 5⅜ × 8½.
24522-5 Pa. $4.50

THE EXPLORATION OF THE COLORADO RIVER AND ITS CANYONS, J. W. Powell. Full text of Powell's 1,000-mile expedition down the fabled Colorado in 1869. Superb account of terrain, geology, vegetation, Indians, famine, mutiny, treacherous rapids, mighty canyons, during exploration of last unknown part of continental U.S. 400pp. 5⅜ × 8½. 20094-9 Pa. $6.95

HISTORY OF PHILOSOPHY, Julián Marías. Clearest one-volume history on the market. Every major philosopher and dozens of others, to Existentialism and later. 505pp. 5⅜ × 8½. 21739-6 Pa. $9.95

ALL ABOUT LIGHTNING, Martin A. Uman. Highly readable non-technical survey of nature and causes of lightning, thunderstorms, ball lightning, St. Elmo's Fire, much more. Illustrated. 192pp. 5⅜ × 8½. 25237-X Pa. $5.95

SAILING ALONE AROUND THE WORLD, Captain Joshua Slocum. First man to sail around the world, alone, in small boat. One of great feats of seamanship told in delightful manner. 67 illustrations. 294pp. 5⅜ × 8½. 20326-3 Pa. $4.95

LETTERS AND NOTES ON THE MANNERS, CUSTOMS AND CONDITIONS OF THE NORTH AMERICAN INDIANS, George Catlin. Classic account of life among Plains Indians: ceremonies, hunt, warfare, etc. 312 plates. 572pp. of text. 6⅛ × 9¼. 22118-0, 22119-9 Pa. Two-vol. set $15.90

ALASKA: The Harriman Expedition, 1899, John Burroughs, John Muir, et al. Informative, engrossing accounts of two-month, 9,000-mile expedition. Native peoples, wildlife, forests, geography, salmon industry, glaciers, more. Profusely illustrated. 240 black-and-white line drawings. 124 black-and-white photographs. 3 maps. Index. 576pp. 5⅜ × 8½. 25109-8 Pa. $11.95

THE BOOK OF BEASTS: Being a Translation from a Latin Bestiary of the Twelfth Century, T. H. White. Wonderful catalog real and fanciful beasts: manticore, griffin, phoenix, amphivius, jaculus, many more. White's witty erudite commentary on scientific, historical aspects. Fascinating glimpse of medieval mind. Illustrated. 296pp. 5⅜ × 8¼. (Available in U.S. only) 24609-4 Pa. $5.95

FRANK LLOYD WRIGHT: ARCHITECTURE AND NATURE With 160 Illustrations, Donald Hoffmann. Profusely illustrated study of influence of nature—especially prairie—on Wright's designs for Fallingwater, Robie House, Guggenheim Museum, other masterpieces. 96pp. 9¼ × 10¾. 25098-9 Pa. $7.95

FRANK LLOYD WRIGHT'S FALLINGWATER, Donald Hoffmann. Wright's famous waterfall house: planning and construction of organic idea. History of site, owners, Wright's personal involvement. Photographs of various stages of building. Preface by Edgar Kaufmann, Jr. 100 illustrations. 112pp. 9¼ × 10. 23671-4 Pa. $7.95

YEARS WITH FRANK LLOYD WRIGHT: Apprentice to Genius, Edgar Tafel. Insightful memoir by a former apprentice presents a revealing portrait of Wright the man, the inspired teacher, the greatest American architect. 372 black-and-white illustrations. Preface. Index. vi + 228pp. 8¼ × 11. 24801-1 Pa. $9.95

THE STORY OF KING ARTHUR AND HIS KNIGHTS, Howard Pyle. Enchanting version of King Arthur fable has delighted generations with imaginative narratives of exciting adventures and unforgettable illustrations by the author. 41 illustrations. xviii + 313pp. 6⅛ × 9¼. 21445-1 Pa. $6.50

THE GODS OF THE EGYPTIANS, E. A. Wallis Budge. Thorough coverage of numerous gods of ancient Egypt by foremost Egyptologist. Information on evolution of cults, rites and gods; the cult of Osiris; the Book of the Dead and its rites; the sacred animals and birds; Heaven and Hell; and more. 956pp. 6⅛ × 9¼. 22055-9, 22056-7 Pa., Two-vol. set $21.90

A THEOLOGICO-POLITICAL TREATISE, Benedict Spinoza. Also contains unfinished *Political Treatise*. Great classic on religious liberty, theory of government on common consent. R. Elwes translation. Total of 421pp. 5⅜ × 8½. 20249-6 Pa. $6.95

INCIDENTS OF TRAVEL IN CENTRAL AMERICA, CHIAPAS, AND YUCATAN, John L. Stephens. Almost single-handed discovery of Maya culture; exploration of ruined cities, monuments, temples; customs of Indians. 115 drawings. 892pp. 5⅜ × 8½. 22404-X, 22405-8 Pa., Two-vol. set $15.90

LOS CAPRICHOS, Francisco Goya. 80 plates of wild, grotesque monsters and caricatures. Prado manuscript included. 183pp. 6⅝ × 9⅝. 22384-1 Pa. $4.95

AUTOBIOGRAPHY: The Story of My Experiments with Truth, Mohandas K. Gandhi. Not hagiography, but Gandhi in his own words. Boyhood, legal studies, purification, the growth of the Satyagraha (nonviolent protest) movement. Critical, inspiring work of the man who freed India. 480pp. 5⅜ × 8½. (Available in U.S. only) 24593-4 Pa. $6.95

ILLUSTRATED DICTIONARY OF HISTORIC ARCHITECTURE, edited by Cyril M. Harris. Extraordinary compendium of clear, concise definitions for over 5,000 important architectural terms complemented by over 2,000 line drawings. Covers full spectrum of architecture from ancient ruins to 20th-century Modernism. Preface. 592pp. 7½ × 9⅜. 24444-X Pa. $15.95

THE NIGHT BEFORE CHRISTMAS, Clement Moore. Full text, and woodcuts from original 1848 book. Also critical, historical material. 19 illustrations. 40pp. 4⅝ × 6. 22797-9 Pa. $2.50

THE LESSON OF JAPANESE ARCHITECTURE: 165 Photographs, Jiro Harada. Memorable gallery of 165 photographs taken in the 1930's of exquisite Japanese homes of the well-to-do and historic buildings. 13 line diagrams. 192pp. 8⅜ × 11¼. 24778-3 Pa. $8.95

THE AUTOBIOGRAPHY OF CHARLES DARWIN AND SELECTED LETTERS, edited by Francis Darwin. The fascinating life of eccentric genius composed of an intimate memoir by Darwin (intended for his children); commentary by his son, Francis; hundreds of fragments from notebooks, journals, papers; and letters to and from Lyell, Hooker, Huxley, Wallace and Henslow. xi + 365pp. 5⅜ × 8. 20479-0 Pa. $6.95

WONDERS OF THE SKY: Observing Rainbows, Comets, Eclipses, the Stars and Other Phenomena, Fred Schaaf. Charming, easy-to-read poetic guide to all manner of celestial events visible to the naked eye. Mock suns, glories, Belt of Venus, more. Illustrated. 299pp. 5¼ × 8¼. 24402-4 Pa. $7.95

BURNHAM'S CELESTIAL HANDBOOK, Robert Burnham, Jr. Thorough guide to the stars beyond our solar system. Exhaustive treatment. Alphabetical by constellation: Andromeda to Cetus in Vol. 1; Chamaeleon to Orion in Vol. 2; and Pavo to Vulpecula in Vol. 3. Hundreds of illustrations. Index in Vol. 3. 2,000pp. 6⅛ × 9¼. 23567-X, 23568-8, 23673-0 Pa., Three-vol. set $38.85

STAR NAMES: Their Lore and Meaning, Richard Hinckley Allen. Fascinating history of names various cultures have given to constellations and literary and folkloristic uses that have been made of stars. Indexes to subjects. Arabic and Greek names. Biblical references. Bibliography. 563pp. 5⅜ × 8½. 21079-0 Pa. $7.95

THIRTY YEARS THAT SHOOK PHYSICS: The Story of Quantum Theory, George Gamow. Lucid, accessible introduction to influential theory of energy and matter. Careful explanations of Dirac's anti-particles, Bohr's model of the atom, much more. 12 plates. Numerous drawings. 240pp. 5⅜ × 8½. 24895-X Pa. $5.95

CHINESE DOMESTIC FURNITURE IN PHOTOGRAPHS AND MEASURED DRAWINGS, Gustav Ecke. A rare volume, now affordably priced for antique collectors, furniture buffs and art historians. Detailed review of styles ranging from early Shang to late Ming. Unabridged republication. 161 black-and-white drawings, photos. Total of 224pp. 8⅜ × 11¼. (Available in U.S. only) 25171-3 Pa. $12.95

VINCENT VAN GOGH: A Biography, Julius Meier-Graefe. Dynamic, penetrating study of artist's life, relationship with brother, Theo, painting techniques, travels, more. Readable, engrossing. 160pp. 5⅜ × 8½. (Available in U.S. only) 25253-1 Pa. $3.95

HOW TO WRITE, Gertrude Stein. Gertrude Stein claimed anyone could understand her unconventional writing—here are clues to help. Fascinating improvisations, language experiments, explanations illuminate Stein's craft and the art of writing. Total of 414pp. 4⅜ × 6⅜. 23144-5 Pa. $5.95

ADVENTURES AT SEA IN THE GREAT AGE OF SAIL: Five Firsthand Narratives, edited by Elliot Snow. Rare true accounts of exploration, whaling, shipwreck, fierce natives, trade, shipboard life, more. 33 illustrations. Introduction. 353pp. 5⅜ × 8½. 25177-2 Pa. $7.95

THE HERBAL OR GENERAL HISTORY OF PLANTS, John Gerard. Classic descriptions of about 2,850 plants—with over 2,700 illustrations—includes Latin and English names, physical descriptions, varieties, time and place of growth, more. 2,706 illustrations. xlv + 1,678pp. 8½ × 12¼. 23147-X Cloth. $75.00

DOROTHY AND THE WIZARD IN OZ, L. Frank Baum. Dorothy and the Wizard visit the center of the Earth, where people are vegetables, glass houses grow and Oz characters reappear. Classic sequel to *Wizard of Oz*. 256pp. 5⅜ × 8.
24714-7 Pa. $4.95

SONGS OF EXPERIENCE: Facsimile Reproduction with 26 Plates in Full Color, William Blake. This facsimile of Blake's original "Illuminated Book" reproduces 26 full-color plates from a rare 1826 edition. Includes "The Tyger," "London," "Holy Thursday," and other immortal poems. 26 color plates. Printed text of poems. 48pp. 5¼ × 7. 24636-1 Pa. $3.50

SONGS OF INNOCENCE, William Blake. The first and most popular of Blake's famous "Illuminated Books," in a facsimile edition reproducing all 31 brightly colored plates. Additional printed text of each poem. 64pp. 5¼ × 7.
22764-2 Pa. $3.50

PRECIOUS STONES, Max Bauer. Classic, thorough study of diamonds, rubies, emeralds, garnets, etc.: physical character, occurrence, properties, use, similar topics. 20 plates, 8 in color. 94 figures. 659pp. 6⅛ × 9¼.
21910-0, 21911-9 Pa., Two-vol. set $15.90

ENCYCLOPEDIA OF VICTORIAN NEEDLEWORK, S. F. A. Caulfeild and Blanche Saward. Full, precise descriptions of stitches, techniques for dozens of needlecrafts—most exhaustive reference of its kind. Over 800 figures. Total of 679pp. 8⅛ × 11. Two volumes. Vol. 1 22800-2 Pa. $11.95
Vol. 2 22801-0 Pa. $11.95

THE MARVELOUS LAND OF OZ, L. Frank Baum. Second Oz book, the Scarecrow and Tin Woodman are back with hero named Tip, Oz magic. 136 illustrations. 287pp. 5⅜ × 8½. 20692-0 Pa. $5.95

WILD FOWL DECOYS, Joel Barber. Basic book on the subject, by foremost authority and collector. Reveals history of decoy making and rigging, place in American culture, different kinds of decoys, how to make them, and how to use them. 140 plates. 156pp. 7⅞ × 10¾. 20011-6 Pa. $8.95

HISTORY OF LACE, Mrs. Bury Palliser. Definitive, profusely illustrated chronicle of lace from earliest times to late 19th century. Laces of Italy, Greece, England, France, Belgium, etc. Landmark of needlework scholarship. 266 illustrations. 672pp. 6⅛ × 9¼. 24742-2 Pa. $14.95

ILLUSTRATED GUIDE TO SHAKER FURNITURE, Robert Meader. All furniture and appurtenances, with much on unknown local styles. 235 photos. 146pp. 9 × 12. 22819-3 Pa. $7.95

WHALE SHIPS AND WHALING: A Pictorial Survey, George Francis Dow. Over 200 vintage engravings, drawings, photographs of barks, brigs, cutters, other vessels. Also harpoons, lances, whaling guns, many other artifacts. Comprehensive text by foremost authority. 207 black-and-white illustrations. 288pp. 6 × 9. 24808-9 Pa. $8.95

THE BERTRAMS, Anthony Trollope. Powerful portrayal of blind self-will and thwarted ambition includes one of Trollope's most heartrending love stories. 497pp. 5⅜ × 8½. 25119-5 Pa. $9.95

ADVENTURES WITH A HAND LENS, Richard Headstrom. Clearly written guide to observing and studying flowers and grasses, fish scales, moth and insect wings, egg cases, buds, feathers, seeds, leaf scars, moss, molds, ferns, common crystals, etc.—all with an ordinary, inexpensive magnifying glass. 209 exact line drawings aid in your discoveries. 220pp. 5⅜ × 8½. 23330-8 Pa. $4.95

RODIN ON ART AND ARTISTS, Auguste Rodin. Great sculptor's candid, wide-ranging comments on meaning of art; great artists; relation of sculpture to poetry, painting, music; philosophy of life, more. 76 superb black-and-white illustrations of Rodin's sculpture, drawings and prints. 119pp. 8⅝ × 11¼. 24487-3 Pa. $6.95

FIFTY CLASSIC FRENCH FILMS, 1912–1982: A Pictorial Record, Anthony Slide. Memorable stills from Grand Illusion, Beauty and the Beast, Hiroshima, Mon Amour, many more. Credits, plot synopses, reviews, etc. 160pp. 8¼ × 11. 25256-6 Pa. $11.95

THE PRINCIPLES OF PSYCHOLOGY, William James. Famous long course complete, unabridged. Stream of thought, time perception, memory, experimental methods; great work decades ahead of its time. 94 figures. 1,391pp. 5⅜ × 8½. 20381-6, 20382-4 Pa., Two-vol. set $23.90

BODIES IN A BOOKSHOP, R. T. Campbell. Challenging mystery of blackmail and murder with ingenious plot and superbly drawn characters. In the best tradition of British suspense fiction. 192pp. 5⅜ × 8½. 24720-1 Pa. $3.95

CALLAS: PORTRAIT OF A PRIMA DONNA, George Jellinek. Renowned commentator on the musical scene chronicles incredible career and life of the most controversial, fascinating, influential operatic personality of our time. 64 black-and-white photographs. 416pp. 5⅜ × 8¼. 25047-4 Pa. $8.95

GEOMETRY, RELATIVITY AND THE FOURTH DIMENSION, Rudolph Rucker. Exposition of fourth dimension, concepts of relativity as Flatland characters continue adventures. Popular, easily followed yet accurate, profound. 141 illustrations. 133pp. 5⅜ × 8½. 23400-2 Pa. $3.95

HOUSEHOLD STORIES BY THE BROTHERS GRIMM, with pictures by Walter Crane. 53 classic stories—Rumpelstiltskin, Rapunzel, Hansel and Gretel, the Fisherman and his Wife, Snow White, Tom Thumb, Sleeping Beauty, Cinderella, and so much more—lavishly illustrated with original 19th century drawings. 114 illustrations. x + 269pp. 5⅜ × 8½. 21080-4 Pa. $4.95

SUNDIALS, Albert Waugh. Far and away the best, most thorough coverage of ideas, mathematics concerned, types, construction, adjusting anywhere. Over 100 illustrations. 230pp. 5⅜ × 8½. 22947-5 Pa. $4.95

PICTURE HISTORY OF THE NORMANDIE: With 190 Illustrations, Frank O. Braynard. Full story of legendary French ocean liner: Art Deco interiors, design innovations, furnishings, celebrities, maiden voyage, tragic fire, much more. Extensive text. 144pp. 8⅞ × 11¾. 25257-4 Pa. $9.95

THE FIRST AMERICAN COOKBOOK: A Facsimile of "American Cookery," 1796, Amelia Simmons. Facsimile of the first American-written cookbook published in the United States contains authentic recipes for colonial favorites—pumpkin pudding, winter squash pudding, spruce beer, Indian slapjacks, and more. Introductory Essay and Glossary of colonial cooking terms. 80pp. 5⅜ × 8½. 24710-4 Pa. $3.50

101 PUZZLES IN THOUGHT AND LOGIC, C. R. Wylie, Jr. Solve murders and robberies, find out which fishermen are liars, how a blind man could possibly identify a color—purely by your own reasoning! 107pp. 5⅜ × 8½. 20367-0 Pa. $2.50

THE BOOK OF WORLD-FAMOUS MUSIC—CLASSICAL, POPULAR AND FOLK, James J. Fuld. Revised and enlarged republication of landmark work in musico-bibliography. Full information about nearly 1,000 songs and compositions including first lines of music and lyrics. New supplement. Index. 800pp. 5⅜ × 8¼. 24857-7 Pa. $14.95

ANTHROPOLOGY AND MODERN LIFE, Franz Boas. Great anthropologist's classic treatise on race and culture. Introduction by Ruth Bunzel. Only inexpensive paperback edition. 255pp. 5⅜ × 8½. 25245-0 Pa. $5.95

THE TALE OF PETER RABBIT, Beatrix Potter. The inimitable Peter's terrifying adventure in Mr. McGregor's garden, with all 27 wonderful, full-color Potter illustrations. 55pp. 4¼ × 5½. (Available in U.S. only) 22827-4 Pa. $1.75

THREE PROPHETIC SCIENCE FICTION NOVELS, H. G. Wells. *When the Sleeper Wakes, A Story of the Days to Come* and *The Time Machine* (full version). 335pp. 5⅜ × 8½. (Available in U.S. only) 20605-X Pa. $6.95

APICIUS COOKERY AND DINING IN IMPERIAL ROME, edited and translated by Joseph Dommers Vehling. Oldest known cookbook in existence offers readers a clear picture of what foods Romans ate, how they prepared them, etc. 49 illustrations. 301pp. 6⅛ × 9¼. 23563-7 Pa. $7.95

SHAKESPEARE LEXICON AND QUOTATION DICTIONARY, Alexander Schmidt. Full definitions, locations, shades of meaning of every word in plays and poems. More than 50,000 exact quotations. 1,485pp. 6½ × 9¼. 22726-X, 22727-8 Pa., Two-vol. set $29.90

THE WORLD'S GREAT SPEECHES, edited by Lewis Copeland and Lawrence W. Lamm. Vast collection of 278 speeches from Greeks to 1970. Powerful and effective models; unique look at history. 842pp. 5⅜ × 8½. 20468-5 Pa. $11.95

THE BLUE FAIRY BOOK, Andrew Lang. The first, most famous collection, with many familiar tales: Little Red Riding Hood, Aladdin and the Wonderful Lamp, Puss in Boots, Sleeping Beauty, Hansel and Gretel, Rumpelstiltskin; 37 in all. 138 illustrations. 390pp. 5⅝ × 8½. 21437-0 Pa. $6.95

THE STORY OF THE CHAMPIONS OF THE ROUND TABLE, Howard Pyle. Sir Launcelot, Sir Tristram and Sir Percival in spirited adventures of love and triumph retold in Pyle's inimitable style. 50 drawings, 31 full-page. xviii + 329pp. 6½ × 9¼. 21883-X Pa. $6.95

AUDUBON AND HIS JOURNALS, Maria Audubon. Unmatched two-volume portrait of the great artist, naturalist and author contains his journals, an excellent biography by his granddaughter, expert annotations by the noted ornithologist, Dr. Elliott Coues, and 37 superb illustrations. Total of 1,200pp. 5⅜ × 8.
Vol. I 25143-8 Pa. $8.95
Vol. II 25144-6 Pa. $8.95

GREAT DINOSAUR HUNTERS AND THEIR DISCOVERIES, Edwin H. Colbert. Fascinating, lavishly illustrated chronicle of dinosaur research, 1820's to 1960. Achievements of Cope, Marsh, Brown, Buckland, Mantell, Huxley, many others. 384pp. 5¼ × 8¼. 24701-5 Pa. $7.95

THE TASTEMAKERS, Russell Lynes. Informal, illustrated social history of American taste 1850's–1950's. First popularized categories Highbrow, Lowbrow, Middlebrow. 129 illustrations. New (1979) afterword. 384pp. 6 × 9.
23993-4 Pa. $8.95

DOUBLE CROSS PURPOSES, Ronald A. Knox. A treasure hunt in the Scottish Highlands, an old map, unidentified corpse, surprise discoveries keep reader guessing in this cleverly intricate tale of financial skullduggery. 2 black-and-white maps. 320pp. 5⅜ × 8½. (Available in U.S. only) 25032-6 Pa. $5.95

AUTHENTIC VICTORIAN DECORATION AND ORNAMENTATION IN FULL COLOR: 46 Plates from "Studies in Design," Christopher Dresser. Superb full-color lithographs reproduced from rare original portfolio of a major Victorian designer. 48pp. 9¼ × 12¼. 25083-0 Pa. $7.95

PRIMITIVE ART, Franz Boas. Remains the best text ever prepared on subject, thoroughly discussing Indian, African, Asian, Australian, and, especially, Northern American primitive art. Over 950 illustrations show ceramics, masks, totem poles, weapons, textiles, paintings, much more. 376pp. 5⅜ × 8. 20025-6 Pa. $6.95

SIDELIGHTS ON RELATIVITY, Albert Einstein. Unabridged republication of two lectures delivered by the great physicist in 1920–21. *Ether and Relativity* and *Geometry and Experience.* Elegant ideas in non-mathematical form, accessible to intelligent layman. vi + 56pp. 5⅜ × 8½. 24511-X Pa. $2.95

THE WIT AND HUMOR OF OSCAR WILDE, edited by Alvin Redman. More than 1,000 ripostes, paradoxes, wisecracks: Work is the curse of the drinking classes, I can resist everything except temptation, etc. 258pp. 5⅜ × 8½. 20602-5 Pa. $4.50

ADVENTURES WITH A MICROSCOPE, Richard Headstrom. 59 adventures with clothing fibers, protozoa, ferns and lichens, roots and leaves, much more. 142 illustrations. 232pp. 5⅜ × 8½. 23471-1 Pa. $3.95

PLANTS OF THE BIBLE, Harold N. Moldenke and Alma L. Moldenke. Standard reference to all 230 plants mentioned in Scriptures. Latin name, biblical reference, uses, modern identity, much more. Unsurpassed encyclopedic resource for scholars, botanists, nature lovers, students of Bible. Bibliography. Indexes. 123 black-and-white illustrations. 384pp. 6 × 9. 25069-5 Pa. $8.95

FAMOUS AMERICAN WOMEN: A Biographical Dictionary from Colonial Times to the Present, Robert McHenry, ed. From Pocahontas to Rosa Parks, 1,035 distinguished American women documented in separate biographical entries. Accurate, up-to-date data, numerous categories, spans 400 years. Indices. 493pp. 6½ × 9¼. 24523-3 Pa. $9.95

THE FABULOUS INTERIORS OF THE GREAT OCEAN LINERS IN HISTORIC PHOTOGRAPHS, William H. Miller, Jr. Some 200 superb photographs capture exquisite interiors of world's great "floating palaces"—1890's to 1980's: *Titanic, Ile de France, Queen Elizabeth, United States, Europa,* more. Approx. 200 black-and-white photographs. Captions. Text. Introduction. 160pp. 8⅞ × 11¾. 24756-2 Pa. $9.95

THE GREAT LUXURY LINERS, 1927-1954: A Photographic Record, William H. Miller, Jr. Nostalgic tribute to heyday of ocean liners. 186 photos of Ile de France, Normandie, Leviathan, Queen Elizabeth, United States, many others. Interior and exterior views. Introduction. Captions. 160pp. 9 × 12. 24056-8 Pa. $10.95

A NATURAL HISTORY OF THE DUCKS, John Charles Phillips. Great landmark of ornithology offers complete detailed coverage of nearly 200 species and subspecies of ducks: gadwall, sheldrake, merganser, pintail, many more. 74 full-color plates, 102 black-and-white. Bibliography. Total of 1,920pp. 8⅜ × 11¼. 25141-1, 25142-X Cloth. Two-vol. set $100.00

THE SEAWEED HANDBOOK: An Illustrated Guide to Seaweeds from North Carolina to Canada, Thomas F. Lee. Concise reference covers 78 species. Scientific and common names, habitat, distribution, more. Finding keys for easy identification. 224pp. 5⅜ × 8½. 25215-9 Pa. $5.95

THE TEN BOOKS OF ARCHITECTURE: The 1755 Leoni Edition, Leon Battista Alberti. Rare classic helped introduce the glories of ancient architecture to the Renaissance. 68 black-and-white plates. 336pp. 8⅜ × 11¼. 25239-6 Pa. $14.95

MISS MACKENZIE, Anthony Trollope. Minor masterpieces by Victorian master unmasks many truths about life in 19th-century England. First inexpensive edition in years. 392pp. 5⅜ × 8½. 25201-9 Pa. $7.95

THE RIME OF THE ANCIENT MARINER, Gustave Doré, Samuel Taylor Coleridge. Dramatic engravings considered by many to be his greatest work. The terrifying space of the open sea, the storms and whirlpools of an unknown ocean, the ice of Antarctica, more—all rendered in a powerful, chilling manner. Full text. 38 plates. 77pp. 9¼ × 12. 22305-1 Pa. $4.95

THE EXPEDITIONS OF ZEBULON MONTGOMERY PIKE, Zebulon Montgomery Pike. Fascinating first-hand accounts (1805-6) of exploration of Mississippi River, Indian wars, capture by Spanish dragoons, much more. 1,088pp. 5⅜ × 8½. 25254-X, 25255-8 Pa. Two-vol. set $23.90

A CONCISE HISTORY OF PHOTOGRAPHY: Third Revised Edition, Helmut Gernsheim. Best one-volume history—camera obscura, photochemistry, daguerreotypes, evolution of cameras, film, more. Also artistic aspects—landscape, portraits, fine art, etc. 281 black-and-white photographs. 26 in color. 176pp. 8⅜ × 11¼. 25128-4 Pa. $13.95

THE DORÉ BIBLE ILLUSTRATIONS, Gustave Doré. 241 detailed plates from the Bible: the Creation scenes, Adam and Eve, Flood, Babylon, battle sequences, life of Jesus, etc. Each plate is accompanied by the verses from the King James version of the Bible. 241pp. 9 × 12. 23004-X Pa. $8.95

HUGGER-MUGGER IN THE LOUVRE, Elliot Paul. Second Homer Evans mystery-comedy. Theft at the Louvre involves sleuth in hilarious, madcap caper. "A knockout."—Books. 336pp. 5⅜ × 8½. 25185-3 Pa. $5.95

FLATLAND, E. A. Abbott. Intriguing and enormously popular science-fiction classic explores the complexities of trying to survive as a two-dimensional being in a three-dimensional world. Amusingly illustrated by the author. 16 illustrations. 103pp. 5⅜ × 8½. 20001-9 Pa. $2.25

THE HISTORY OF THE LEWIS AND CLARK EXPEDITION, Meriwether Lewis and William Clark, edited by Elliott Coues. Classic edition of Lewis and Clark's day-by-day journals that later became the basis for U.S. claims to Oregon and the West. Accurate and invaluable geographical, botanical, biological, meteorological and anthropological material. Total of 1,508pp. 5⅜ × 8½.
21268-8, 21269-6, 21270-X Pa. Three-vol. set $26.85

LANGUAGE, TRUTH AND LOGIC, Alfred J. Ayer. Famous, clear introduction to Vienna, Cambridge schools of Logical Positivism. Role of philosophy, elimination of metaphysics, nature of analysis, etc. 160pp. 5⅜ × 8½. (Available in U.S. and Canada only) 20010-8 Pa. $2.95

MATHEMATICS FOR THE NONMATHEMATICIAN, Morris Kline. Detailed, college-level treatment of mathematics in cultural and historical context, with numerous exercises. For liberal arts students. Preface. Recommended Reading Lists. Tables. Index. Numerous black-and-white figures. xvi + 641pp. 5⅜ × 8½.
24823-2 Pa. $11.95

28 SCIENCE FICTION STORIES, H. G. Wells. Novels, *Star Begotten* and *Men Like Gods,* plus 26 short stories: "Empire of the Ants," "A Story of the Stone Age," "The Stolen Bacillus," "In the Abyss," etc. 915pp. 5⅜ × 8½. (Available in U.S. only)
20265-8 Cloth. $10.95

HANDBOOK OF PICTORIAL SYMBOLS, Rudolph Modley. 3,250 signs and symbols, many systems in full; official or heavy commercial use. Arranged by subject. Most in Pictorial Archive series. 143pp. 8⅛ × 11. 23357-X Pa. $6.95

INCIDENTS OF TRAVEL IN YUCATAN, John L. Stephens. Classic (1843) exploration of jungles of Yucatan, looking for evidences of Maya civilization. Travel adventures, Mexican and Indian culture, etc. Total of 669pp. 5⅜ × 8½.
20926-1, 20927-X Pa., Two-vol. set $9.90

DEGAS: An Intimate Portrait, Ambroise Vollard. Charming, anecdotal memoir by famous art dealer of one of the greatest 19th-century French painters. 14 black-and-white illustrations. Introduction by Harold L. Van Doren. 96pp. 5⅜ × 8½.
25131-4 Pa. $3.95

PERSONAL NARRATIVE OF A PILGRIMAGE TO ALMANDINAH AND MECCAH, Richard Burton. Great travel classic by remarkably colorful personality. Burton, disguised as a Moroccan, visited sacred shrines of Islam, narrowly escaping death. 47 illustrations. 959pp. 5⅜ × 8½. 21217-3, 21218-1 Pa., Two-vol. set $19.90

PHRASE AND WORD ORIGINS, A. H. Holt. Entertaining, reliable, modern study of more than 1,200 colorful words, phrases, origins and histories. Much unexpected information. 254pp. 5⅜ × 8½. 20758-7 Pa. $5.95

THE RED THUMB MARK, R. Austin Freeman. In this first Dr. Thorndyke case, the great scientific detective draws fascinating conclusions from the nature of a single fingerprint. Exciting story, authentic science. 320pp. 5⅜ × 8½. (Available in U.S. only) 25210-8 Pa. $5.95

AN EGYPTIAN HIEROGLYPHIC DICTIONARY, E. A. Wallis Budge. Monumental work containing about 25,000 words or terms that occur in texts ranging from 3000 B.C. to 600 A.D. Each entry consists of a transliteration of the word, the word in hieroglyphs, and the meaning in English. 1,314pp. 6⅞ × 10.
23615-3, 23616-1 Pa., Two-vol. set $31.90

THE COMPLEAT STRATEGYST: Being a Primer on the Theory of Games of Strategy, J. D. Williams. Highly entertaining classic describes, with many illustrated examples, how to select best strategies in conflict situations. Prefaces. Appendices. xvi + 268pp. 5⅜ × 8½. 25101-2 Pa. $5.95

THE ROAD TO OZ, L. Frank Baum. Dorothy meets the Shaggy Man, little Button-Bright and the Rainbow's beautiful daughter in this delightful trip to the magical Land of Oz. 272pp. 5⅜ × 8. 25208-6 Pa. $4.95

POINT AND LINE TO PLANE, Wassily Kandinsky. Seminal exposition of role of point, line, other elements in non-objective painting. Essential to understanding 20th-century art. 127 illustrations. 192pp. 6½ × 9¼. 23808-3 Pa. $4.95

LADY ANNA, Anthony Trollope. Moving chronicle of Countess Lovel's bitter struggle to win for herself and daughter Anna their rightful rank and fortune—perhaps at cost of sanity itself. 384pp. 5⅜ × 8½. 24669-8 Pa. $8.95

EGYPTIAN MAGIC, E. A. Wallis Budge. Sums up all that is known about magic in Ancient Egypt: the role of magic in controlling the gods, powerful amulets that warded off evil spirits, scarabs of immortality, use of wax images, formulas and spells, the secret name, much more. 253pp. 5⅜ × 8½. 22681-6 Pa. $4.50

THE DANCE OF SIVA, Ananda Coomaraswamy. Preeminent authority unfolds the vast metaphysic of India: the revelation of her art, conception of the universe, social organization, etc. 27 reproductions of art masterpieces. 192pp. 5⅜ × 8½.
24817-8 Pa. $5.95

CHRISTMAS CUSTOMS AND TRADITIONS, Clement A. Miles. Origin, evolution, significance of religious, secular practices. Caroling, gifts, yule logs, much more. Full, scholarly yet fascinating; non-sectarian. 400pp. 5⅜ × 8½.
23354-5 Pa. $6.50

THE HUMAN FIGURE IN MOTION, Eadweard Muybridge. More than 4,500 stopped-action photos, in action series, showing undraped men, women, children jumping, lying down, throwing, sitting, wrestling, carrying, etc. 390pp. 7⅞ × 10⅝.
20204-6 Cloth. $21.95

THE MAN WHO WAS THURSDAY, Gilbert Keith Chesterton. Witty, fast-paced novel about a club of anarchists in turn-of-the-century London. Brilliant social, religious, philosophical speculations. 128pp. 5⅜ × 8½. 25121-7 Pa. $3.95

A CEZANNE SKETCHBOOK: Figures, Portraits, Landscapes and Still Lifes, Paul Cezanne. Great artist experiments with tonal effects, light, mass, other qualities in over 100 drawings. A revealing view of developing master painter, precursor of Cubism. 102 black-and-white illustrations. 144pp. 8¾ × 6⅜. 24790-2 Pa. $5.95

AN ENCYCLOPEDIA OF BATTLES: Accounts of Over 1,560 Battles from 1479 B.C. to the Present, David Eggenberger. Presents essential details of every major battle in recorded history, from the first battle of Megiddo in 1479 B.C. to Grenada in 1984. List of Battle Maps. New Appendix covering the years 1967–1984. Index. 99 illustrations. 544pp. 6½ × 9¼. 24913-1 Pa. $14.95

AN ETYMOLOGICAL DICTIONARY OF MODERN ENGLISH, Ernest Weekley. Richest, fullest work, by foremost British lexicographer. Detailed word histories. Inexhaustible. Total of 856pp. 6½ × 9¼.
21873-2, 21874-0 Pa., Two-vol. set $17.00

WEBSTER'S AMERICAN MILITARY BIOGRAPHIES, edited by Robert McHenry. Over 1,000 figures who shaped 3 centuries of American military history. Detailed biographies of Nathan Hale, Douglas MacArthur, Mary Hallaren, others. Chronologies of engagements, more. Introduction. Addenda. 1,033 entries in alphabetical order. xi + 548pp. 6½ × 9¼. (Available in U.S. only)
24758-9 Pa. $11.95

LIFE IN ANCIENT EGYPT, Adolf Erman. Detailed older account, with much not in more recent books: domestic life, religion, magic, medicine, commerce, and whatever else needed for complete picture. Many illustrations. 597pp. 5⅜ × 8½.
22632-8 Pa. $8.95

HISTORIC COSTUME IN PICTURES, Braun & Schneider. Over 1,450 costumed figures shown, covering a wide variety of peoples: kings, emperors, nobles, priests, servants, soldiers, scholars, townsfolk, peasants, merchants, courtiers, cavaliers, and more. 256pp. 8⅜ × 11¼. 23150-X Pa. $8.95

THE NOTEBOOKS OF LEONARDO DA VINCI, edited by J. P. Richter. Extracts from manuscripts reveal great genius; on painting, sculpture, anatomy, sciences, geography, etc. Both Italian and English. 186 ms. pages reproduced, plus 500 additional drawings, including studies for *Last Supper, Sforza* monument, etc. 860pp. 7⅞ × 10¾. (Available in U.S. only) 22572-0, 22573-9 Pa., Two-vol. set $29.90

THE ART NOUVEAU STYLE BOOK OF ALPHONSE MUCHA: All 72 Plates from "Documents Decoratifs" in Original Color, Alphonse Mucha. Rare copyright-free design portfolio by high priest of Art Nouveau. Jewelry, wallpaper, stained glass, furniture, figure studies, plant and animal motifs, etc. Only complete one-volume edition. 80pp. 9⅜ × 12¼. 24044-4 Pa. $8.95

ANIMALS: 1,419 COPYRIGHT-FREE ILLUSTRATIONS OF MAMMALS, BIRDS, FISH, INSECTS, ETC., edited by Jim Harter. Clear wood engravings present, in extremely lifelike poses, over 1,000 species of animals. One of the most extensive pictorial sourcebooks of its kind. Captions. Index. 284pp. 9 × 12. 23766-4 Pa. $9.95

OBELISTS FLY HIGH, C. Daly King. Masterpiece of American detective fiction, long out of print, involves murder on a 1935 transcontinental flight—"a very thrilling story"—NY Times. Unabridged and unaltered republication of the edition published by William Collins Sons & Co. Ltd., London, 1935. 288pp. 5⅜ × 8½. (Available in U.S. only) 25036-9 Pa. $4.95

VICTORIAN AND EDWARDIAN FASHION: A Photographic Survey, Alison Gernsheim. First fashion history completely illustrated by contemporary photographs. Full text plus 235 photos, 1840–1914, in which many celebrities appear. 240pp. 6½ × 9¼. 24205-6 Pa. $6.95

THE ART OF THE FRENCH ILLUSTRATED BOOK, 1700–1914, Gordon N. Ray. Over 630 superb book illustrations by Fragonard, Delacroix, Daumier, Doré, Grandville, Manet, Mucha, Steinlen, Toulouse-Lautrec and many others. Preface. Introduction. 633 halftones. Indices of artists, authors & titles, binders and provenances. Appendices. Bibliography. 608pp. 8⅜ × 11¼. 25086-5 Pa. $24.95

THE WONDERFUL WIZARD OF OZ, L. Frank Baum. Facsimile in full color of America's finest children's classic. 143 illustrations by W. W. Denslow. 267pp. 5⅜ × 8½. 20691-2 Pa. $5.95

FRONTIERS OF MODERN PHYSICS: New Perspectives on Cosmology, Relativity, Black Holes and Extraterrestrial Intelligence, Tony Rothman, et al. For the intelligent layman. Subjects include: cosmological models of the universe; black holes; the neutrino; the search for extraterrestrial intelligence. Introduction. 46 black-and-white illustrations. 192pp. 5⅜ × 8½. 24587-X Pa. $6.95

THE FRIENDLY STARS, Martha Evans Martin & Donald Howard Menzel. Classic text marshalls the stars together in an engaging, non-technical survey, presenting them as sources of beauty in night sky. 23 illustrations. Foreword. 2 star charts. Index. 147pp. 5⅜ × 8½. 21099-5 Pa. $3.50

FADS AND FALLACIES IN THE NAME OF SCIENCE, Martin Gardner. Fair, witty appraisal of cranks, quacks, and quackeries of science and pseudoscience: hollow earth, Velikovsky, orgone energy, Dianetics, flying saucers, Bridey Murphy, food and medical fads, etc. Revised, expanded In the Name of Science. "A very able and even-tempered presentation."—The New Yorker. 363pp. 5⅜ × 8. 20394-8 Pa. $6.50

ANCIENT EGYPT: ITS CULTURE AND HISTORY, J. E Manchip White. From pre-dynastics through Ptolemies: society, history, political structure, religion, daily life, literature, cultural heritage. 48 plates. 217pp. 5⅜ × 8½. 22548-8 Pa. $5.95

SIR HARRY HOTSPUR OF HUMBLETHWAITE, Anthony Trollope. Incisive, unconventional psychological study of a conflict between a wealthy baronet, his idealistic daughter, and their scapegrace cousin. The 1870 novel in its first inexpensive edition in years. 250pp. 5⅜ × 8½. 24953-0 Pa. $5.95

LASERS AND HOLOGRAPHY, Winston E. Kock. Sound introduction to burgeoning field, expanded (1981) for second edition. Wave patterns, coherence, lasers, diffraction, zone plates, properties of holograms, recent advances. 84 illustrations. 160pp. 5⅜ × 8¼. (Except in United Kingdom) 24041-X Pa. $3.50

INTRODUCTION TO ARTIFICIAL INTELLIGENCE: SECOND, ENLARGED EDITION, Philip C. Jackson, Jr. Comprehensive survey of artificial intelligence—the study of how machines (computers) can be made to act intelligently. Includes introductory and advanced material. Extensive notes updating the main text. 132 black-and-white illustrations. 512pp. 5⅜ × 8½. 24864-X Pa. $8.95

HISTORY OF INDIAN AND INDONESIAN ART, Ananda K. Coomaraswamy. Over 400 illustrations illuminate classic study of Indian art from earliest Harappa finds to early 20th century. Provides philosophical, religious and social insights. 304pp. 6⅝ × 9⅝. 25005-9 Pa. $8.95

THE GOLEM, Gustav Meyrink. Most famous supernatural novel in modern European literature, set in Ghetto of Old Prague around 1890. Compelling story of mystical experiences, strange transformations, profound terror. 13 black-and-white illustrations. 224pp. 5⅜ × 8½. (Available in U.S. only) 25025-3 Pa. $6.95

ARMADALE, Wilkie Collins. Third great mystery novel by the author of *The Woman in White* and *The Moonstone*. Original magazine version with 40 illustrations. 597pp. 5⅜ × 8½. 23429-0 Pa. $9.95

PICTORIAL ENCYCLOPEDIA OF HISTORIC ARCHITECTURAL PLANS, DETAILS AND ELEMENTS: With 1,880 Line Drawings of Arches, Domes, Doorways, Facades, Gables, Windows, etc., John Theodore Haneman. Sourcebook of inspiration for architects, designers, others. Bibliography. Captions. 141pp. 9 × 12. 24605-1 Pa. $6.95

BENCHLEY LOST AND FOUND, Robert Benchley. Finest humor from early 30's, about pet peeves, child psychologists, post office and others. Mostly unavailable elsewhere. 73 illustrations by Peter Arno and others. 183pp. 5⅜ × 8½. 22410-4 Pa. $3.95

ERTÉ GRAPHICS, Erté. Collection of striking color graphics: *Seasons, Alphabet, Numerals, Aces* and *Precious Stones*. 50 plates, including 4 on covers. 48pp. 9⅜ × 12¼. 23580-7 Pa. $6.95

THE JOURNAL OF HENRY D. THOREAU, edited by Bradford Torrey, F. H. Allen. Complete reprinting of 14 volumes, 1837–61, over two million words; the sourcebooks for *Walden*, etc. Definitive. All original sketches, plus 75 photographs. 1,804pp. 8½ × 12¼. 20312-3, 20313-1 Cloth., Two-vol. set $80.00

CASTLES: THEIR CONSTRUCTION AND HISTORY, Sidney Toy. Traces castle development from ancient roots. Nearly 200 photographs and drawings illustrate moats, keeps, baileys, many other features. Caernarvon, Dover Castles, Hadrian's Wall, Tower of London, dozens more. 256pp. 5⅜ × 8¼. 24898-4 Pa. $5.95

CATALOG OF DOVER BOOKS

AMERICAN CLIPPER SHIPS: 1833–1858, Octavius T. Howe & Frederick C. Matthews. Fully-illustrated, encyclopedic review of 352 clipper ships from the period of America's greatest maritime supremacy. Introduction. 109 halftones. 5 black-and-white line illustrations. Index. Total of 928pp. 5⅜ × 8½.
25115-2, 25116-0 Pa., Two-vol. set $17.90

TOWARDS A NEW ARCHITECTURE, Le Corbusier. Pioneering manifesto by great architect, near legendary founder of "International School." Technical and aesthetic theories, views on industry, economics, relation of form to function, "mass-production spirit," much more. Profusely illustrated. Unabridged translation of 13th French edition. Introduction by Frederick Etchells. 320pp. 6⅛ × 9¼. (Available in U.S. only) 25023-7 Pa. $8.95

THE BOOK OF KELLS, edited by Blanche Cirker. Inexpensive collection of 32 full-color, full-page plates from the greatest illuminated manuscript of the Middle Ages, painstakingly reproduced from rare facsimile edition. Publisher's Note. Captions. 32pp. 9⅜ × 12¼. 24345-1 Pa. $4.95

BEST SCIENCE FICTION STORIES OF H. G. WELLS, H. G. Wells. Full novel *The Invisible Man,* plus 17 short stories: "The Crystal Egg," "Aepyornis Island," "The Strange Orchid," etc. 303pp. 5⅜ × 8½. (Available in U.S. only)
21531-8 Pa. $6.95

AMERICAN SAILING SHIPS: Their Plans and History, Charles G. Davis. Photos, construction details of schooners, frigates, clippers, other sailcraft of 18th to early 20th centuries—plus entertaining discourse on design, rigging, nautical lore, much more. 137 black-and-white illustrations. 240pp. 6⅛ × 9¼.
24658-2 Pa. $6.95

ENTERTAINING MATHEMATICAL PUZZLES, Martin Gardner. Selection of author's favorite conundrums involving arithmetic, money, speed, etc., with lively commentary. Complete solutions. 112pp. 5⅜ × 8½. 25211-6 Pa. $2.95

THE WILL TO BELIEVE, HUMAN IMMORTALITY, William James. Two books bound together. Effect of irrational on logical, and arguments for human immortality. 402pp. 5⅜ × 8½. 20291-7 Pa. $7.50

THE HAUNTED MONASTERY and THE CHINESE MAZE MURDERS, Robert Van Gulik. 2 full novels by Van Gulik continue adventures of Judge Dee and his companions. An evil Taoist monastery, seemingly supernatural events; overgrown topiary maze that hides strange crimes. Set in 7th-century China. 27 illustrations. 328pp. 5⅜ × 8½. 23502-5 Pa. $5.95

CELEBRATED CASES OF JUDGE DEE (DEE GOONG AN), translated by Robert Van Gulik. Authentic 18th-century Chinese detective novel; Dee and associates solve three interlocked cases. Led to Van Gulik's own stories with same characters. Extensive introduction. 9 illustrations. 237pp. 5⅜ × 8½.
23337-5 Pa. $4.95

Prices subject to change without notice.

Available at your book dealer or write for free catalog to Dept. GI, Dover Publications, Inc., 31 East 2nd St., Mineola, N.Y. 11501. Dover publishes more than 175 books each year on science, elementary and advanced mathematics, biology, music, art, literary history, social sciences and other areas.